THE ULTIMATE BASKETBALL BOOK

A Complete Shooting Guide

By Frank L. Wright

Published by

Sierra Vista Publications, Crystal Bay, Nevada
A division of Alpine Sports U.S.A.

First Edition Published in ©2003 FL Wright
Second Edition Published in ©2007 FL Wright

Printed in Hong Kong
Designed by Andrew D. Garcia
Photographs courtesy Alpine Sports

For Information:
Sierra Vista Publications
P.O. Box 186 Crystal Bay, Nevada 89402
E-mail: alpinesports@earthlink.net

Library of Congress Cataloging-in Publication-Data
70030500000395686323
Wright, Wright

ISBN 0-9711314-9-X

Forward

This book will give the serious basketball player a clear and precise blueprint for success. If a player follows the directions and examples in this book they will learn the skills necessary to compete at the highest competitive level. A strong work ethic complemented by many hours of practice will help to ensure success. Many players do not realize their full potential because the concepts and drills provided in this book are not readily available. Most athletes only receive bits and pieces of needed instruction as they grow and develop, resulting in countless hours spent practicing incorrect fundamentals. They get good at doing some things totally wrong and perfection becomes impossible.

Basketball players who have the skills needed to compete on varsity teams do not develop those skills overnight. It takes time and many hours of work to perfect these skills. If a player is blessed with a natural ability for the game, it goes without saying that they have a tremendous advantage at a young age. But they tend to rely on their ability and don't always work to develop skills needed later in their careers. Many players develop bad habits that are very hard to break *(some are impossible to fix)* as they get older. Players cannot change their natural athleticism, but any player can learn how to shoot a basketball correctly and become extremely good at other fundamentals. Becoming a great player requires a combination of many factors, including a solid work ethic, sharp shooting skills, strong fundamentals and a great attitude. Practicing the skills found in this book will help a player build a solid fundamental base and many of the lessons contained herein will help young athletes in other sports as well.

Table of Contents

Chapter Five

Chapter Six

Chapter Seven

Chapter Eight

Introduction

This book was written with the primary intent to standardize and clarify the correct way to shoot a basketball as well as to offer players a complete program to develop competitive offensive and defensive skills. Since its inception, the game of basketball has seen many shooting techniques evolve, most of which are fundamentally incorrect. As a result, very few high school, college, or professional coaches have sophisticated shooting programs. Most coaches in America have had very little instruction on the correct way to shoot a basketball. Because the practice of shooting is not standardized, players across America have a wide variety of shooting techniques. Players have developed many different shooting styles and most of them are incorrect. Over time a player can become very good at shooting the wrong way. The wide disparity in shooting forms makes it difficult to teach other players.

Aside from having proper instruction, there are many views as to what makes a great shooter. Consistency is a trait that can be taught, but the willingness to learn must come from within. A good work ethic and positive attitude greatly influence a player's potential. Combined, these characteristics will enable a player to dramatically improve their shooting percentages. A coach who has learned the basics of shooting can be a great asset to a developing player.

The standard accepted percentage for a player shooting outside the key is around forty percent. This standard is too low; sixty percent is where the standard should be set. With proper instruction and practice, this measure is attainable.

Developing strong individual offensive basketball skills is very difficult when you do not practice sound fundamental techniques. Young players begin shooting on ten foot baskets, and use balls that are too big for them to handle. They immediately begin reinforcing bad habits by trying to shoot the bigger ball at a very high target. These bad habits evolve and tend to stay with the players during their careers. If a golfer were to start at a young age with an adult set of clubs, they would develop very poor techniques. The same holds true for young basketball players. It is very important in basketball, as well as golf or any other sport, to develop proper skills early in life. As a basketball player continues to grow and develop it becomes difficult to change bad habits and to replace them with proper shooting techniques.

This book contains a collection of training techniques and instruction about basketball. If properly learned and thoroughly practiced, this information will help a player develop superior skills that will set him or her apart from the competition.

Chapter ONE

Fundamentals Needed To Create A Perfect SHOT

The Shot

This is a step-by-step process that will lead to a perfect shooting style if practiced correctly.

The Basics

The first thing a player should do is learn how to hold the ball. A right handed player should place their right hand firmly in the center of the ball, with their fingers spread out slightly across the ball. The middle and index finger are the keys to an accurate shot. The thumb, much like the left hand, is used only to control the ball. The left hand should be placed on the side of the ball where it only acts to control the ball – for our purposes, it is called the help hand. Many players will mistakenly place their help hand too high or too far forward and the help hand will actually block the shot.

To Target.

There should be a little space between the palm of the hand and the basketball.

These two fingers' tips should go directly toward the basket.

The index and middle fingers (***photo B***) are going to direct the path of the ball toward the center of the rim. The finger tips are the most critical part of the shot. They must pass in a direct line toward the basket.

Help hand.

Help hand on the side of the ball.

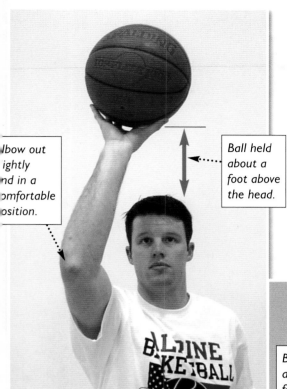

bow out ightly nd in a omfortable osition.

Ball held about a foot above the head.

This angle shows the view a player has looking directly at the target *(basket)*. The right elbow *(shooting elbow)* is slightly turned out in a natural and comfortable position. The left hand *(help hand)* is not interfering with the shot. The help hand is keeping the ball steady, and allows the shooting hand to follow through. The shoulders are square to the basket.

Notice the position of the shooting elbow. It is slightly bent, and in a comfortable position.

Do not allow ball to go behind forehead.

To Target.

Ball held about a foot above the head.

The ball should be held about one foot above the forehead. The elbow should be bent slightly out in a comfortable position. The position of the elbow is a controversial issue with many coaches. Having the elbow "locked-in" and pointing straight down is uncomfortable and unnatural with regards to the arm movement and follow through. Having the elbow pointing straight down locks up the follow-through. At the other extreme, if the elbow is too far out the hand is forced to come across the ball, causing a very erratic shot. Therefore a slight angle is ideal.

The ball is held out in front of the forehead to give the player a clear, open view of the target. The higher the ball is held, the better. The ball should never be brought back behind the head. Bringing the ball behind your forehead will create unnecessary movement in the shoulders and forearms, causing accuracy to suffer. Players tend to drop the release point lower and lower as they become tired causing them to miss shots. The ball is filled with air and is not heavy, but the natural instinct is to begin to bring the ball down as one gets fatigued.

The position of the shoulders and the feet are critical to the success of the shot. This player is square to the basket as the right foot is slightly forward and the left foot is back. The feet are a comfortable shoulder's width apart. The right foot points directly at the basket.

The Understanding Of Touch When Shooting

The most important element of a successful shot understanding the "feel" or "touch." This "touch" comes from the fingertips as the ball is released.

Place your fingertips and hand next to someone else's, *(as shown in photo A)*. Apply pressure at the fingertips. The other person should apply the same pressure. The index and middle finger should provide the thrust of power; this same power would be the guiding power for the basketball. The index and middle finger would continue towards the basket, followed by the wrist and forearm.

If you feel the palm of the other person's hand touch your hand first, then they are shooting incorrectly. Using too much palm is the most common problem with poor shooters. The finger tips must "go" through the ball first.

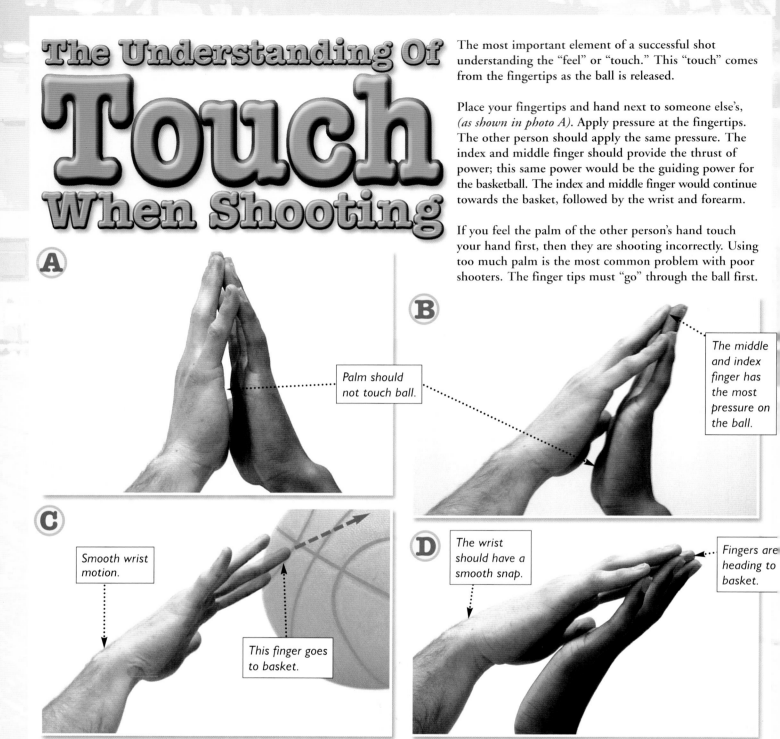

A

Palm should not touch ball.

B

The middle and index finger has the most pressure on the ball.

C

Smooth wrist motion.

This finger goes to basket.

D

The wrist should have a smooth snap.

Fingers are heading to basket.

The wrist is very important for successful shot. It must be smooth and fluid, never rigid or "jerky."

The wrist is beginning to snap, following the fingertips to the basket. The forearm also follows the fingertips. The palm of the shooting hand is not involved and is not part of the shot. If the palm or heal of the shooting hand touches the ball at any time during the course of the shot it will produce a very erratic shot. The fingertips should continue toward the basket and snap down as the ball is released. This will create a backwards rotation spin on the ball as it travels toward the target.

The Shooting Window

This is the view a basketball player creates while shooting. The shooting window is a triangle formed between the elbows and the basketball. In order to be a great shooter, the basketball player needs to create a window to see the target. If a player does not have a clear vision towards the basket, shooting percentages will drop drastically. If the shooter creates a perfect shooting window his shooting percentages will improve significantly. The "pure shooters" in the game of basketball all have a wide-open shooting window. If you do not have a solid shooting window, it will be impossible to develop a consistent shot.

Notice now both eyes have a clear view of the basket.

The ball is held high above the top of the head *(at least one foot above the forehead)*. The ball should be out in front, never behind the forehead. The elbows create a natural triangle that gives the shooter a clear unobstructed view of the basket. This shooting window is absolutely needed to become a great shooter. Both eyes have to have a clear vision toward the basket.

The shoulders and feet must be square to the basket, with the right foot *(or left, depending on which hand you are shooting with)* slightly forward.

A rear view of the shooting window: The help hand is on the left-hand side of the ball and the players head is right in the middle of the shooting window, or triangle. Nothing should be blocking the view of the shooter.

The Follow-Through

Release

When taking the shot, the ball should roll off the fingertips. The fingertips are the only part of the hand that should touch the ball. If you feel the palm of your hand going through the ball first, you are shooting with your shoulder and forearm. Shooting this way will never lead to a consistent and accurate shot. The hand needs to be behind the ball, not underneath the ball.

The Wrist

The wrist is one of the most important parts of the shot. It must be flexible. A stiff wrist will not allow you to follow-through. As the ball is shot, the middle and index finger work together with the wrist to create backspin on the ball. This is also called ball **rotation**.

The Finish

The Follow-Through: A Rear View

This player has lost direction of the shooting hand. The right shoulder is pointed towards the left. The right arm is blocking the vision of the shooter. These types of shooting mistakes are common in most basketball players because they are not aware they are shooting this way. Accuracy suffers when players shoot this way.

Arm is too far to the left.

Vision is blocked. Shoulder and arm are blocking players vision.

WRONG

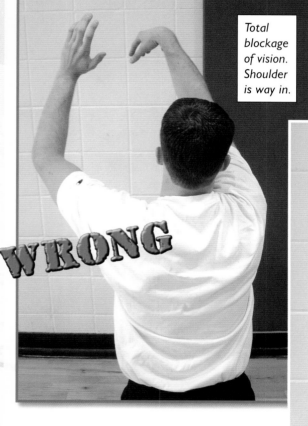

Total blockage of vision. Shoulder is way in.

WRONG

Wrist is snapping towards target, very flexible.

Nice shooting window. Total vision.

Square shoulders.

RIGHT

The follow-through should look like this. Notice how the shoulders are square to the target. The shooting hand is finishing down and in a straight line. The vision of the shooter is not obstructed.

The Finish

The finish to the follow-through is as important as the release itself. The fingertips and the wrist complete the shot. The arm will follow in a natural fluid flow. The help hand will drop to the outside away from the vision of the shooter. The hips, shoulders and feet should be square to the basket.

Help hand is not in the way of shot.

Middle and index finger have a straight path to the basket.

Perfect shooting window.

When shooting, it is important for the fingertips, especially those at the middle and index fingers, to go through the middle of the ball – heading directly at the basket. Notice the player has completed the release and the middle and index fingers are heading toward the basket. The wrist has followed the fingertips through the ball. The help hand or left hand is dropping off to the side. The shoulders are square to the basket.

Body Alignment

It is very important to make sure the right side of your body is aligned with the basket. This photo shows the player slightly leaning to the right. The right foot is inside the right shoulder. The shooting hand however is lined up and square with the right foot.

Shooting window partially blocked by elbow on shooting hand.

Shooting window.

Shoulders should be square to basket.

Feet facing basket.

This angle shows that the shooting hand and the right foot are slightly out of alignment. The ball could be moved to the right an inch or two. Small adjustments will lead to dramatically improved results in shooting ability.

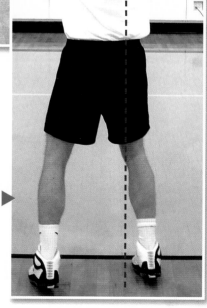

Drawing an imaginary line down the middle of the basket to the floor allows you to see how the body can be out of alignment and can lead to missed shots. This player is lined up almost perfectly.

Zone One

When learning to shoot a basketball correctly it is important that a player start right in front of the basket, about one foot back from the rim and directly in front. This is where adjustments can be made in regard to body alignment, and position of the head and shoulders. The middle and index finger on the shooting hand should be in the middle of the ball pointing directly to the middle of the basket. The ball should be held high above the head and out in front of the forehead. The left hand should be located on the side of the ball.

A

Perfect position of the "help" hand.

Notice how the shooter's shoulder is square to the basket.

ZONE ONE

B

ZONE 1

Zone Two

This zone is located about two steps back from the rim directly in front of the basket. A shooter should be able to see the target through the shooting triangle. This shot, much like zone one, should be a finesse shot using the finger tips and the snap of the wrist. Make sure the body and feet are square to the basket before shooting.

C

ZONE 2

Helpful Hint:

Alternate shots at each locations. Take a shot in **Zone 2**, then **Zone 3**, then **Zone 4**, then back to **Zone 1**. This will teach you how to vary your shot from different locations.

D

ZONE 3

Shooting Zones

No Shot Zone

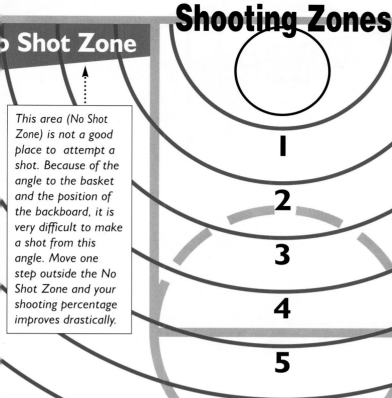

This area (No Shot Zone) is not a good place to attempt a shot. Because of the angle to the basket and the position of the backboard, it is very difficult to make a shot from this angle. Move one step outside the No Shot Zone and your shooting percentage improves drastically.

1
2
3
4
5
6
7

Chart To Help You Check Your Shot

	Goal	Shots	Make
ZONE 1	95	*Out of* 100	
ZONE 2	95	*Out of* 100	
ZONE 3	95	*Out of* 100	
ZONE 4	90	*Out of* 100	
ZONE 5	85	*Out of* 100	
ZONE 6	80	*Out of* 100	
ZONE 7	75	*Out of* 100	

s a player moves backwards from zone o zone consistency and accuracy must be ressed. This player is now in **Zone 4** nd is demonstrating the same form as nown in **Zone 1**. The player moves to **Zone 5** he is now about to the free-throw ne. If the player who works his way to is point, and maintains the same ooting skills as demonstrated in **Zone 1**, e player's free throw shooting ercentage should improve drastically. **Zone 6** is between the free-throw line nd the three point arc. This is where ost players begin to break form. Because f the added distance, most players will egin to change their shots. This is a mmon problem, and takes a very isciplined player to avoid developing bad abits. A player must maintain the same ooting form used in **Zone 1** when ooting in **Zone 6** and **Zone 7**. A layer should be able to make 25 shots in row from **Zone 1** before moving to **Zone 2**. Then making 25 in a row before oving to **Zone 3** and continue to **Zone 7**. Sometimes it will take a player x months to reach **Zone 6** or **7**.

ZONE 4

FREE THROW RANGE
ZONE 5

ZONE 6

3 PT. RANGE
ZONE 7

Lining Up The Feet

The yellow line shows how the feet should be lined up prior to shooting. The right foot is slightly forward and the left foot is slightly back. The feet are about a foot apart. The weight of the player should be on the balls of the feet. It is important to not lean back or have weight on the heels. Many players do not think about the alignment of the feet when shooting. Yet, if your feet are not squared to the basket, the shoulders and the hips are probably not lined up either.

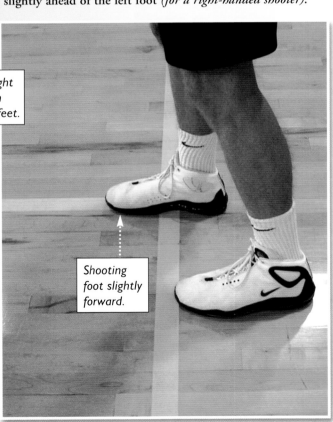

The feet are heading straight forward. The right foot is slightly ahead of the left foot *(for a right-handed shooter)*.

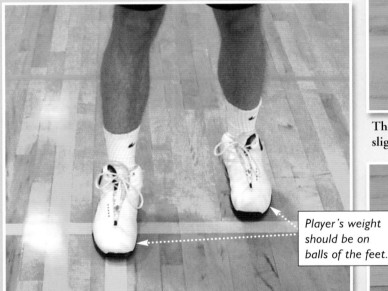

Player's weight should be on balls of the feet.

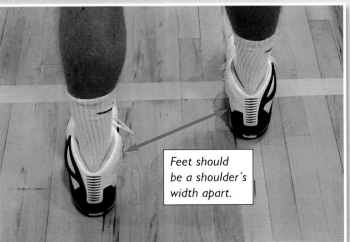

Feet should be a shoulder's width apart.

Shooting foot slightly forward.

Shooting From The Weak Side Of The Court

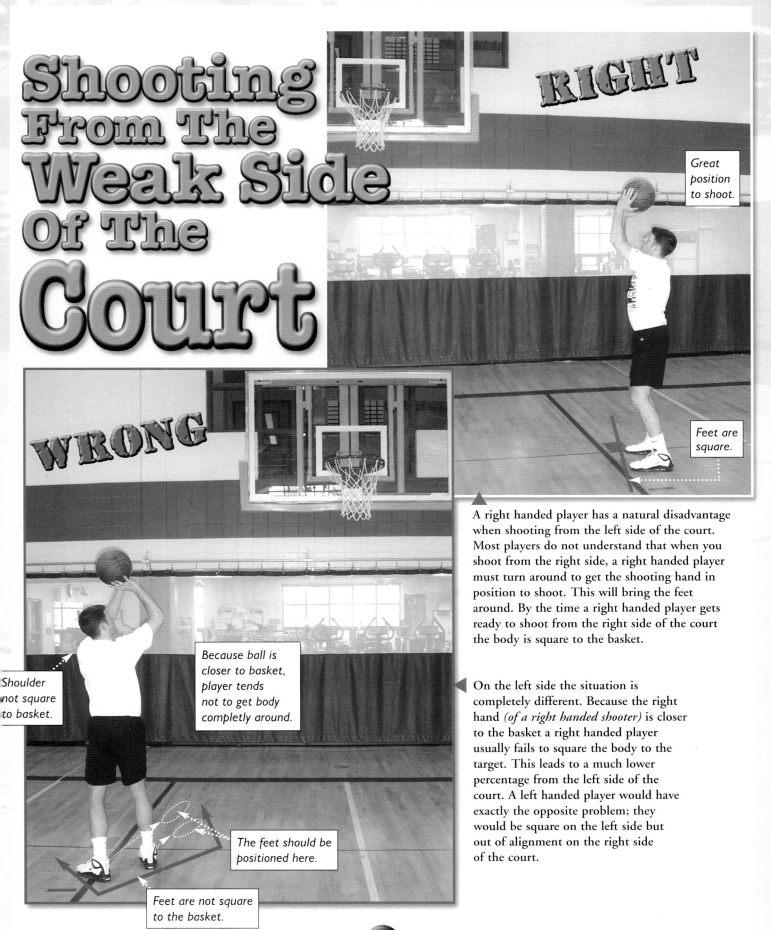

RIGHT

Great position to shoot.

Feet are square.

WRONG

Shoulder not square to basket.

Because ball is closer to basket, player tends not to get body completly around.

The feet should be positioned here.

Feet are not square to the basket.

A right handed player has a natural disadvantage when shooting from the left side of the court. Most players do not understand that when you shoot from the right side, a right handed player must turn around to get the shooting hand in position to shoot. This will bring the feet around. By the time a right handed player gets ready to shoot from the right side of the court the body is square to the basket.

On the left side the situation is completely different. Because the right hand *(of a right handed shooter)* is closer to the basket a right handed player usually fails to square the body to the target. This leads to a much lower percentage from the left side of the court. A left handed player would have exactly the opposite problem; they would be square on the left side but out of alignment on the right side of the court.

HOW TO Shoot A Free-Throw

Shooting a free throw should be done exactly the same way as any other shot.

When shooting a free throw you should develop a routine that has the following basic principles:

1   Walk to the line and find the center. A small finish nail usually indicates the spot. (When the lines are painted on the court, this nail is used as a reference spot – so the nail should line up directly with the basket).

2   Place your right toe directly behind the line at the point where the nail is. The left foot should be lined up on the nail for left handed shooters.

3   Some players choose to take a few dribbles to relax and get comfortable before beginning the shot. This is fine as long as you are consistent in your routine.

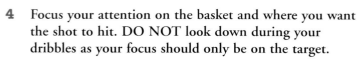
Place your right toe behind the finish nail.

4   Focus your attention on the basket and where you want the shot to hit. DO NOT look down during your dribbles as your focus should only be on the target.

5   Bring the ball up to the shooting position. Make sure your middle and index fingers are heading directly towards the basket.

6   Bend the knees and shoot the ball with a comfortable rhythm.

7   Pay attention to where the shot hits on the rim so adjustments can be made for the second attempt.

8   Your feet should not leave the ground, nor should they move after you have shot the ball (i.e. don't lean forward or backward).

9   After the shot, be ready to get the rebound or get back on defense!

Knees slightly bent.

Weight on balls of feet.

Hints for
Free throw perfection:

- Never walk away from the free throw line between free throws attempts so you don't alter your alignment. The first shot is a good indicator and can show you how to make adjustments for the second shot.

- Timing, rhythm and rotation will make for a smooth and sweet free throw.

- Don't worry about retrieving the ball after the first attempt – the referee will get the ball to you. Stay focused and look at the target to get your shot lined up.

- Your socks are a good place to dry off your hands before shooting a free throw.

- Never slap or "hi-five" a teammate's hand after you make the first shot. It interferes with your focus and could potentially mess up your second shot.

- Make sure the middle and index fingers are heading toward the basket.

- If the first free throw is short, make sure the second one is well above the rim.

Lay-Ups

The basic fundamental rule of a lay-up is the following: If you are right handed, the right hand will go high towards the basket. The right knee will lift high towards the basket as well. The left foot will be the takeoff foot.

Over Hand Lay-up

Left hand.
Left knee.

Over Hand Lay-up

Right hand.
Right knee.

The lay-up is probably one of the most misunderstood shots in basketball. There are two types of lay-ups. The underhand lay-up and the overhand lay-up. The underhand lay-up, when being defended by a defensive player, is a lower percentage shot because it is easy to block. The overhand lay-up is the most common and most accurate. Most players cannot shoot the lay-up from both sides of the basket. A right-handed player usually cannot make a left-handed lay-up with the same accuracy that they have from the right side. A right handed player who has not learned how to shoot a left handed lay-up will cheat and use their right hand to shoot from the left side of the court. This practice brings the ball to the side the defense is on and makes it difficult to get the shot off.

Under Hand Lay-up

Hitting The Target When Shooting A Lay-Up

The target area for a lay-up should be about a foot and a half above the rim *(the upper corner of the square on the backboard)*. Many players, especially those on an open court fast break lay-up, will bury the ball into the bottom of the rim. Coaches will get angry at the player for missing the shot. The reason they hit the bottom of the rim is simple, they hit exactly where they intended to aim. The player needs to train his/her eyes to hit the target above the rim.

Shot high on glass, away from rim and bounces to middle of the basket.

Perfect spot to hit on layup.

RIGHT

WRONG

Wrong foot on take off.

Shot buried into rim.

COMMON MISTAKE.

The worst spot to hit on a layup.

WRONG

25

The Jump Shot

Timing – Rhythm – Rotation.
Getting off the ground to shoot a jump shot.

It is important to release the shot at the top of your jump. The feet and shoulders should be square to the basket As you leave the floor it is important to keep your head and eyes focused at the target or basket. If you shoot on the way up the ball will carry and usually you get a hard shot. If you shoot on the way down you will come up short. Timing, rhythm, and shot rotation are extremely important. Start practicing this shot by standing still and facing the basket. Get the ball high and jump. Shoot the ball at the top of the jump.

The Funnel Effect

"As a shooter gets farther away from the basket, the flaws in the shooters shooting style becomes greater."

The flaws or mistakes a shooter makes while shooting is magnified as the shooter gets farther away from the basket. Shooters mistakes are less noticeable close to the basket. If a baseball pitcher throws a curve ball two feet from the catcher the human eye can not detect the ball bending. But when the same pitch is thrown from 60 feet away, you can detect the bend, or curve in the path of the ball. The same holds true for a basketball player when shooting. The closer to the target, the less noticeable the bend in the ball. When shooting the same shot at the three point line you will notice the shot's trajectory. A player should focus in making sure their shot has a smooth and consistent trajectory that is without any curves or crooked movements.

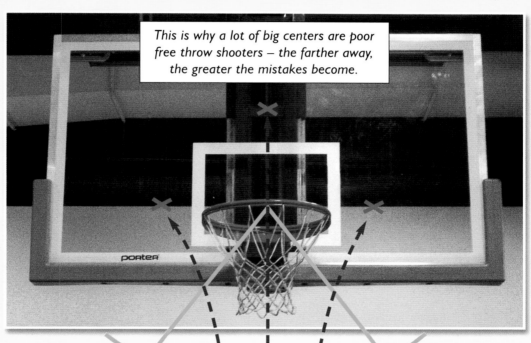

This is why a lot of big centers are poor free throw shooters — the farther away, the greater the mistakes become.

You don't notice crooked shots in Zone 1-2-3.

ZONE 1

ZONE 2   ZONE 2

WRONG → RIGHT ← WRONG

ZONE 3

The shooting hand turning to the left or right at the end of the shot is a very common mistake in poor shooters.

ZONE 4   ZONE 4

In Zone 4, you can really detect shooting flaws.

The Baby Hook Shot

This shot is probably the most effective shot in basketball

Very few high school and college players use this shot in games because many coaches don't teach the shot or encourage its use. Yet, when used, percentages are exceptionally high. The reasons for not having a player with the shot in his arsenal of shots is confusing. Much like the sky-hook, coaches have forgotten how valuable the baby hook shot can be. The baby hook shot is extremely difficult to stop. Once a shooter sets up to shoot the shot the defense is at an extreme disadvantage. Usually the shooter will get the shot off or get the foul. Being able to use both your left and right hands in shooting the baby hook gives the shooter a tremendous offensive advantage.

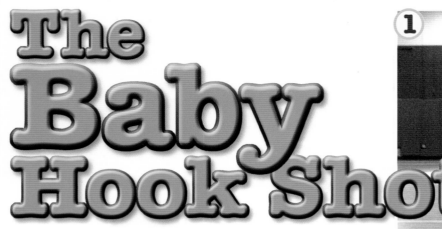

Setting up the Baby Hook Shot.

Player's eyes are focused on target.

Deciding on shooting to the left or right depends on the location or the defensive player.

Here the player catches the ball with his back to the basket.

A

As the player turns towards the basket, he keeps the ball high.

B

Left hand is protecting the ball, similar to the lay-up. The right foot and right hand operate together.

This hand clears a path to basket.

The knee lifts high.

Shooter gets high off ball of left foot.

C

It is very important to get the shot off high above the head.

Help hand clears path to basket.

5

Wrist snaps, middle and index finger toward basket.

6

Wrist has snapped and followed the ball to the basket.

7

Shot Analysis

Where the ball hits on the rim can teach the shooter what is wrong with his or her shot.

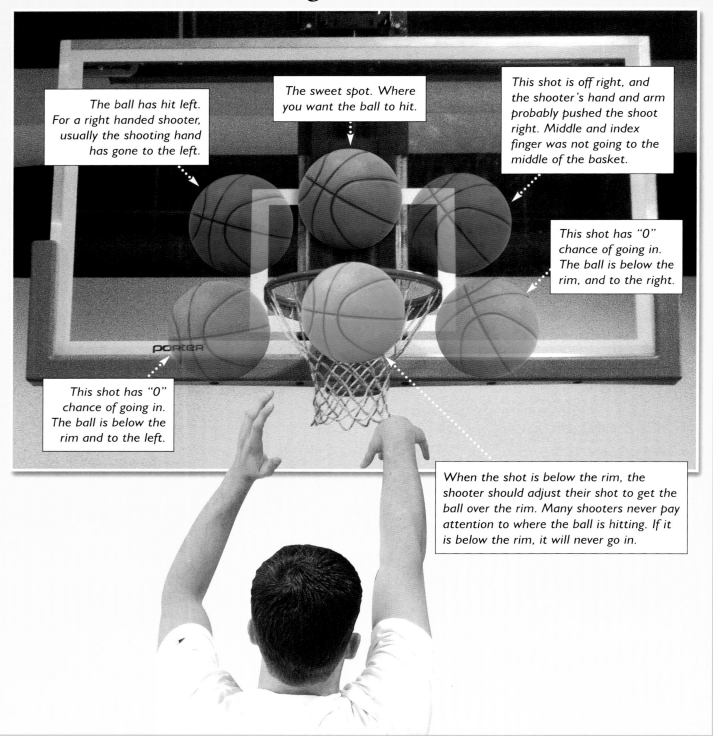

The ball has hit left. For a right handed shooter, usually the shooting hand has gone to the left.

The sweet spot. Where you want the ball to hit.

This shot is off right, and the shooter's hand and arm probably pushed the shoot right. Middle and index finger was not going to the middle of the basket.

This shot has "0" chance of going in. The ball is below the rim, and to the right.

This shot has "0" chance of going in. The ball is below the rim and to the left.

When the shot is below the rim, the shooter should adjust their shot to get the ball over the rim. Many shooters never pay attention to where the ball is hitting. If it is below the rim, it will never go in.

Why You Should Not Shoot A Finger Roll

The best shot is from the right or left side using the glass.

The basket will protect shots from being blocked.

Finger rolls are shots that are taken from in front of the rim. It is a lower percentage shot. Take the shot from either the right or left side of the basket. When the ball hits the glass, it will significantly increase the accuracy of short shots.

The biggest problem with finger rolls is:

A Ball hits front of rim and bounces away.

B Ball carries over rim, hits the back of the rim and bounces away.

WRONG WAY SHOOTERS

"Hip Chucker"

"Cross Eyed Jack"

3. This player has the ball too far on the left side. The feet are not square to the basket. The right arm is blocking the view of the target. The hips are turned sideways and the help hand is under the ball. This shot has very little chance of going into the basket. If it does go in the basket it would be more luck than skill.

1. This player has the ball too low; the defense could easily take the ball, or put a hand in the area where the shooter would bring the ball up to shoot.

"Ear Shot"

2. The shooter has the ball on the side of his head, the shooting hand is under the ball and he will push or shove the ball much like a shot putter in track. Great for distance, but this method gives little to accuracy. The help hand is behind the ball as well, and probably will interfere with the shot's direction of travel.

"Flying Eagle"

4. Both hands are shooting the ball, and both hands are going away from the basket. This is a shot used in the early days of basketball. Because both hands are going different directions the ball tends to head to the basket. This was probably one of the more effective shots in the 1940's and 1950's. But it was marginal for developing high shooting percentages.

"Self Destructing"

5. Here the shooter is actually blocking his own shot. The help hand is around and too far in front of the ball. The shooting window is good. But the ball will have a funny rotation because the help hand is in the way. Shooters having this problem will tend to be very erratic and have "streaks" which can't be explained.

"Side Winder"

7. This player is turned to the left, the body is not square to the basket. The player will lose power behind the shot. The farther away from the basket this player gets the tougher the shot becomes.

8. The wrist on the shooting hand is twisted to the left on the follow through. This type of shooter will find most shots hit on the left side of the rim.

"Broken Wing"

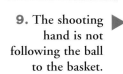

"Two Hand Push"

6. The two hand push. This is easy for the defense to block, not that you would want to, because the shooter probably is going to miss the shot anyway. The ball is too low, both hands are shooting the ball and the ball has to cross the vision of the shooter and the target. As long as you have the time to set up to shoot this shot you will be somewhat successful. But it is a very poor shot for today's game of basketball.

9. The shooting hand is not following the ball to the basket.

"Sharp Right Turn"

"Sharp Right Turn" a rear view"

10. On this shot the player does not have the middle and index finger heading to the basket. The shooting hand is actually heading off to the right of the shooter.

"Magic Cross"

12. Right elbow is too far out and the help hand is across the top of the head. Notice how the shoulders are tilted to the left and not square to the basket.

"Heave Ho"

"Tipsy"

11. This player is off balance; the feet are not helping the shooter with his shot. The shooter is not square to the basket. He might have rushed the shot before getting set to shoot.

"Step Shot"

13. Here the ball is too far behind the player's head. The help hand is placed too far forward. The eyes of the shooter will have to readjust to pick up the flight of the ball as the ball comes back into the shooter's view.

14. This is a player who has the right foot stepping forward. The ball is too low, and the shooting hand is under the ball creating a "shot put" type shot.

"Ankle Kisser"

15. The feet are too close together. The shooter is not balanced and his shot will not have complete power.

"Side Push"

16. The ball is too low, and behind the player's head. This type of shot is very difficult to control. The player will miss more than he makes.

"Cross Over"

"Peek-A-Boo"

"Right Hand Shove"

Notice how the arm is going away from the target.

17. The right elbow is out too far and the shooting hand is across the body to the left side. The shooters vision is totally blocked. This shot is much like #3 but this shooter cannot see the target.

18. The ball is totally blocking the shooter's vision. This player will not see the basket until after the ball is released.

19. The shooting hand and arm are going left of the shooter's body and away from the target. This player will lose power, not to mention accuracy.

"Shoulder Shove"

"Flying Elbow"

"Help Hand Cross-over"

"Sling Shot"

"Peek A Boo" side view

20. A rear view of the shooters hand crossing to the left. The shooter's vision is totally blocked by the right arm. The right shoulder is turning to the left, away from the basket.

21. This player's right elbow is "flying." A shooter having this shot tends to come across the ball. Notice how the shooting hand is turned out and away from the basket.

22. This is rather common. It looks really funny, but many players have this happen to them after the shot. The help hand gets in the way of the shooting hand. The shooting hand is crossing in front of the shooter. This makes for a very eratic shot.

23. The ball is behind the shooter's head. Players who shoot this way usually "sling" the ball. This shot is much like #13 but the help hand is helping to "toss" the ball.

24. The ball is too low and blocking the shooters vision. This shot is very common when players are shooting free throws. The ball is blocking a good look at the basket.

The Ultimate Six-Month Shooting Program

This shooting program, if seriously followed for a period of six months, will lead to the development of outstanding shooting skills.

The best time to develop a basketball shot is during the off-season. This is usually between the months of March to August. If strictly followed, the average shooter will become a very good shooter during the off-season. The program requires serious dedication and intense practice. Each day over the course of the six months, a player should shoot a minimum of 1,000 shots a day. These shots must be completed under a very strict and focused practice environment so a player can develop a true and pure shot. The 1,000 shots or more a day must be attempted while practicing alone or with a partner who is rebounding. Any type of distraction will cause a player to lose focus. A player cannot correctly analyze and evaluate their shooting technique if they are not paying close attention to each and every shot taken.

The following shooting routines will appear to be monotonous and repetitive, but to become a great shooter, following this routine is a necessity. The reason there is a serious lack of good shooters in high school and college today is due to the commitment one must make to become a great shooter. The countless hours spent to develop a complete and correct shooting style is a major deterrent.

The First Month:

All the shots taken during this initial period should be in Zones 1, 2 or 3.

Each shot taken should be measured against the following fundamentals:

1. The ball should be at least one foot above the shooters head and out in front of the forehead.
   (See illustration on page 11)

2. Ball should be rolling off the fingertips with a "backspin" rotation.
   The wrist should snap while the middle and index fingers direct the ball to the basket.

3. The shot should be quick, yet soft.

4. Each shot should be a clean "swish" and not hit the rim.

5. Feet should be facing the basket.

6. Shoulders are square to the basket.

7. Feet on each shot should be square to the basket.

Do not accept a missed shot – find out why you missed and fix the problem.

Suggested Routine

Shoot at least 1,000 shots each day from any spot in zones 1, 2 or 3. Pay close attention to detail. Study each and every shot. See where the shot is hitting the rim and double check all the basic fundamental skills listed above.

*Videotape your shooting sessions each week to see if your shot is fundamentally sound. Keep a copy for future comparison. Over a period of time you will see drastic improvements in your shot. Mistakes are much easier to detect when you videotape and take photos of your shot.

Shoot 100 shots in a row and record how many you make. Keep track of each shot by shooting 100 at a time. This makes it easy to calculate your shooting percentages.

Each night before you go to sleep:

Lie on your back and shoot the basketball up in the air. Because the ball comes right back down you can get off a lot of shots in a short amount of time. You will want to do this until your arm is completely exhausted. Before getting out of bed in the morning, repeat the same exercise. Study the photo to the right, it is important to maintain the correct shooting form.

The Second Month:
Continue shooting 1000 shots per day in zones 1, 2 & 3.

Now begin to pivot after each shot and move to a new location within the three zones. *(See the pivot drills on pages 82-83).* The following skills should be added to your shooting workout.

1. Pivots *(pages 82-83 for full explaination)*

2. Bank shots from zone 1 and 2

3. Lay-ups *(see pages 24-25)*

4. Short jump shot *(see page 26)*

5. Begin to work on the baby hook shot *(refer to pages 28-29)*

The Third Month:

By now you should feel comfortable and begin to shoot further away from the basket. After completing month one and two correctly, you should have built up enough arm strength to move back to zones 4 and 5. A player should have the strength and coordination to confidently shoot from zone 5 by the end of this month. It is critical for the player to work on getting the shot off very quickly. It is okay to practice slowly at first so that form is not compromised. By the 3rd month a player should start shooting quickly to simulate game conditions.

Shooting in Zones 4 and 5

Analyze each shot and pay attention to missed shots *(particularly where they hit the rim or backboard).* If the shot is hitting to the left side you may be pushing the shot too much with your right shoulder and arm. It is a vital to study each and every shot and to demand personal perfection. If you miss, ask yourself why and work diligently to fix the problem.

Shooting Zone

No Shot Zone   No Shot Zone

1
2
3
4
5
6
7

ZONE 4

ZONE

Having a rebounding and shooting partner is a great help during this stage of development. As you shoot and pivot, having someone to rebound for you allows you to get a lot of shots off in a shorter amount of time. The partner can also videotape your shot and subsequent motions (*i.e. pivots, spins, off-the-ball movement*). Continue to shoot at least 1,000 shots a day.

The Fourth Month

The shooter has now passed the halfway point in developing a truly unique shot. If the prior three months directions have been followed, the shooter's accuracy should be around 80% from zones 4 and 5 and about 90% in zones 1, 2 and 3. The fundamentals should be very sound by now. The players feet, shoulders and shooting window should be well established.

At this point it is important to start incorporating the jump shot into the daily routine. Additionally, every shot taken should have a pivot (before or after the shot). Furthermore, it is recommended that you adjust your daily workout to incorporate the following drills:

- Elbow-to-Elbow: 300 shots per day
- Elbow to Baseline: 300 shots per day
- Bow tie drill: 300 shots per day *(See page 120)*

Spin moves, pivots, "ball speed" and a few "pump fakes" should be incorporated. *(Review pages 46, 65, 99-101)*

In addition to the above, you should shoot a minimum of 100 free throws at the end of your workout each day. Practicing free-throws while fatigued is the best way to simulate game circumstances. A player can make 14/15 free-throws in a game, yet still be considered a "goat" if that one missed free-throw is when their team is down by one with no time left on the clock.

The Fifth Month

The footwork of the shooter should be very well-established by this time and he/she should begin working on taking a few dribbles before the shot; begin with one or two dribbles from the top to the key. As the player gets to the area around the free-throw line he/she should stop and shoot a quick, yet well-composed jump shot. This should be done to the right and to the left sides of the key *(in equal amounts to prevent one side from becoming stronger than the other)*. As the player gets comfortable with the timing and coordination, the movement should become very fluid, quick and precise.

Incorporating pivots between a few dribbles and before a jump shot is also strongly recommended at this point. After picking up the dribble and before taking the shot, a player should practice adding some ball speed. With all of these "add-ins" shooting a 1,000 shots is going to take longer and will be more exhausting, but this has to be done to incorporate the lessons of the first four months into game situations.

Halfway through the month the shooter should add pivots to each shot and spin moves to the left and right off the dribble. *(Pages 66-67)*

The Sixth Month

Adding a defensive player to the workout by having someone guard you while you complete your shooting drills is extremely important and effective. Every drill practiced in month 1-5 should be now practiced by having someone play defense. You will experience some difficulty getting your shots off and your shooting percentages will drop significantly. At first you may experience trouble getting the shot off, but as you practice you will find that by using ball speed and pivots it is really easy to shake a defensive player and get your shot off.

Playing in pickup games and full court scrimmages allows you to practice your spin moves, pivots, and ball speed. Attempt to use the hook shot and other shots you have been practicing. Pay attention to those shots that need further work and continue to practice those things that were difficult to execute in game situations.

Chapter TWO

Learning How To TOSS THE ROCK

Passing Skills

There are many different types of passing skills needed to be a complete basketball player.

WRONG

The pass is very difficult to complete.

WRONG

The person catching the ball has to look over his shoulder.

These passes need to be practiced extensively to become an outstanding passer. This chapter explains passing skills and the basic rules that a player should follow to maximize assists and prevent turnovers.

Passing Angles: Never pass to a player who is directly in front of you. Take advantage of the angle. This means creating a triangle between you and the person you are passing to. This diagram *(to the left)* shows a player passing to his teammate directly in front. This is a very difficult pass to complete. The receiving player must catch the pass over his shoulder, which is difficult and awkward.

RIGHT

The greater this distance, the easier the pass becomes.

Here the passer has a much better angle to complete the pass, the receiver is to the right and in front of the passer. By opening the angle, the pass has a much better chance of being caught.

Basic Passes

Chest Pass

This pass is one of the most basic passing forms and the foundation for many other passes. It should be used for close range passes (8 – 15 ft) and used when the defense is not heavily contesting the pass.

Initiate the pass by holding the ball at chest level, with both hands behind the ball. Begin the pass by taking one step forward.

As you are stepping forward, extend the ball away from the chest in the direction you are going to pass the ball.

Notice the position of the hands on the ball. Both hands should be in the same position and the thumbs should be facing each other.

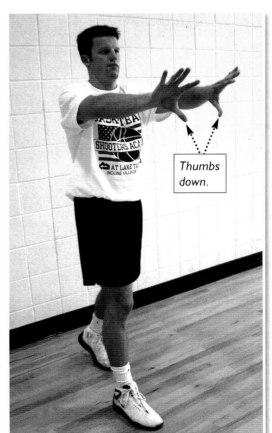

Thumbs down.

After the release, your thumbs should be pointing toward the ground and the ball should be "snapped" quickly toward the intended receiver. The trajectory of the ball should be a straight line.

Overhead Pass

Both hands should be positioned similarly on the ball, as in the chest pass. This pass is used if the defense is up in your face and ready to contest the pass. The trajectory of the ball should be straight like an arrow.

Take one step forward in the direction you are going to pass the ball. *(Note that if the defense is in your face, it may not be possible to take one step into them. Taking a step forward will increase the power behind the pass).*

This pass is great because the passer has total vision of the court.

Start with the ball above the head

Snap the ball towards the intended receiver and after the ball has left your hands, both of your thumbs should be pointed toward the ground – similar to the finishing position of the chest pass.

Bounce Pass

This pass is effective for getting the ball into the post player. To intercept the pass, the defense would have to reach around the intended receiver. This would cause the defensive player to get off balance and they would most likely get called for a foul as they reach around. This pass can also be used for inbounding the ball into heavy defensive traffic.

Begin this pass in the same position as the chest pass.

Take one-step forward in the direction you intend to pass the ball and push the ball forward in a diagonal direction towards the ground.

After the ball is released, the bounce should occur at about two thirds of the total distance of the pass. The remaining 1/3 bounce will be a quick pop up to the intended receiver. Make sure your hands continue in the direction of the pass and snap at the release of the ball. This way, the ball will quickly bounce up towards the receiver and not give the defense the opportunity to pick off the pass.

Behind the back pass

This is an advanced pass that requires many hours of practice prior to its use in a game. This pass is very effective and will easily fool the defense. The best way to practice this is to throw the ball against a target on a wall. This pass usually is thrown over short distances (8 to 15 feet). Once you have mastered this skill, you will be able to add some other exciting passes including the behind the back bounce pass and between the legs bounce pass – all of which may lead to innovative offensive opportunities.

To complete this pass you should be heading in one direction and throwing the ball behind you in a wrap-around manner toward the intended receiver.

After picking up your dribble, initiate the pass by stepping forward and making eye contact with the intended receiver.

Draw a target on wall.

Keep the ball waist high as you begin to bring it around your back.

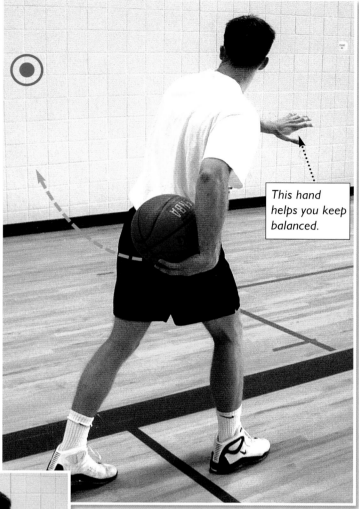

This hand helps you keep balanced.

As you "wrap" the ball around your back you will snap your wrist and allow the ball to slide off the fingertips

Here the ball is released and heading towards the target you have placed on the wall. Accuracy is extremely important when making this pass.

The wrist snaps, and ball should roll off fingers.

Hints:

- Hit the target 100 times with the left hand then hit the target 100 times with the right hand.

- Be able to make this pass off the dribble.

Overhead Pump Fake & Pass

A

Using ball speed, the offensive player is pumping the pass much like a football player would do to isolate a receiver. The pump fake pass will make the defense react and a good fake will make the defensive player lean, and lose their balance.

◄ Here the offensive player is pumping to the right. Notice how the defense is already starting to lean.

B

Center of gravity is leaning to the right.

Using the ball as a decoy, you can usually get the defense to move any direction you choose.

C

By snapping the pass to the left you create passing lanes.

The offensive player is bringing the ball quickly back to the opposite side of his body and the defense is forced to react.

◄ By quickly snaping the ball to the right again the defense will be leaning and out of position.

The Baseball Pass

This pass is thrown exactly like a pitcher would throw a baseball at a batter. This pass is usually used for long passes of least fifteen feet or more. The most common use is out of bound plays going the length of the court. Very few players learn to throw this pass with the same accuracy in both hands. If you know how to use both hands you improve your total passing ability by 50 percent.

Here the player is preparing to throw the baseball pass using his right hand. The left foot is forward and the left hand is extended for balance. The throw should be above the shoulders and the ball will pass right by the players right ear. This is very similar to a football quarterback's pass.

These players are using their left hand to throw the baseball pass. The right hand is out for balance and the right foot is slightly forward.

The best way to practice this pass is against a wall with a target marked on the wall.

Right handed baseball pass.

Developing the Ultimate Baseball Pass:

- Stand 15 feet away from the target. Throw 50 times with your right hand, and 50 times with your left hand

- Move 30 feet from the target. Repeat 50 times with each hand

- Continue to move back to increase accuracy at greater distance

One Handed Reach & Pass TO THE RIGHT

The one-handed reach pass is used to get around the defensive player. It is very easy to use "ball speed" to get the defense to react and then the offensive player will reach and step around the defense. Developing ball speed will help to successfully complete this pass. A player's size is not a limiting factor in completing a good pass.

B

The offensive player snaps the ball and steps to the right placing his right foot past the defense's left foot, while reaching under the defense's left arm.

A

Here the offensive player is beginning to set up the defense. This pass begins with the offensive player quickly pumping the ball to the left.

C

The offensive player is now past the defense. The offensive player begins to reach out with the right hand and begins the pass.

Shoulder is past defense.

Foot steps by defense.

D

Shoulder is behind defensive player.

The offensive player has completely gone past the defense, snapping the pass past the offensive player's left knee. Notice how the left foot is well past the defense.

Foot is by defense.

One Handed Reach & Pass TO THE LEFT

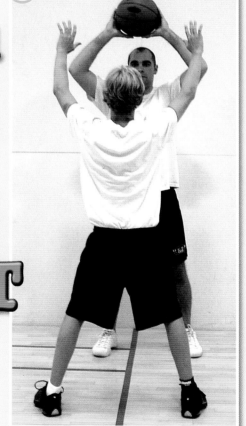

1

The ball is out and away from the defense. Even if the defense reacts by steping back the pass is easily completed.

2

Arm used to clear passing lane.

3

Wrist snaps for crisp pass.

A *Ball fake.*

Set up defense to drop hand.

The Ear Pass

The ear pass is a very effective pass which is impossible to defend against, if executed properly. Using ball speed and quick pivots an offensive player can create a passing lane right by a defenders ear.

B *Snap pass.*

Here the defense is reacting to a pump fake pass to the left and low by the defensive players right knee. The defense will put a hand in the passing lane and try to stop the pass.

The defensive player cannot get his hand back quick enough to stop the pass.

The offensive player quickly brings the ball up and snaps a pass by the ear of the defensive player.

Pass goes by defensive players ear.

C

The defender's hand cannot react fast enough to stop pass. Ball will be past the ear before the defensive player's can reach.

Ear Pass Around The Defense

Fake the low pass. Bring the ball up quickly after the pump fake, then a pass by the defender's ear.

You will need to practice this pass over and over before you would want to use it in a game. But when you have this pass developed it becomes a great offensive weapon.

Snap the ball past the defensive players ear.

The defender is too late to re-act.

Chapter THREE

Ball Handling SKILLS AND DRILLS

Ball Handling

The goal of ball handling is to become "one" with the basketball. A great ball handler will feel more comfortable with a basketball in their hand than any other object. When a player has a basketball in their hand they should feel like they are in a place where they have been a thousand times. A great ball handler will seize a scoring opportunity with a tenacity that will put defensive players at his/her mercy. Comfort, familiarity and confidence with a basketball can only come through countless hours of practice.

Who should be a good ball-handler?

Without qualification, every offensive player from the center to the point guard should command the same skillset. A post player should feel just as comfortable when dribbling and maneuvering while in possession of the ball as the point guard. The post player's capacity for learning the proper ball-handling fundamentals are often overlooked because they are not expected to dribble as much during the course of the game. But time and time again, the lack of basic ball handling and dribbling skills eludes even the most talented post players. Too many crucial "game-deciding" turnovers are attributable to a clumsy post player trying to make the first few dribbles of a fast break. The coach will frenetically scream to get the ball to the "outlets" (i.e. guards) so that he won't "freak out" while the "big man" tries to dribble. This is unacceptable. The "big man" should command the same mastery of ball-handling skills as the point guard.

Underdevelopment begets over dependence.

A common weakness seen in many developing players throughout the junior high/high-school ranks is the over dependence on their strong hand. This weakness is easily identifiable and a smart defensive player will capitalize on it every time. Not developing both hands equally will make a player feel less confident and increase the likelihood of a turnover or a missed scoring opportunity.

What can a player do to improve their ball-handling skills?

There are many exercises and drills that have been modified and taught over the years so that a player can correct bad habits, eliminate over dependence on one hand and increase confidence. In this section, we hope to explain a broad cross section of the many drills and exercises that can help you develop fundamental ball handling skills.

How much time should I spend on ball-handling each day?

Assuming that you can allocate 3 hours to practicing your skills each day, you should spend approximately 30 minutes to one hour on ball handling drills.

Basic Ball Handling Drills

Around the Waist:

This is one of the essential building blocks for a complete ball handling skillset. Pass the ball from one hand to the other as you move it around your waist. Keep the ball as close to the body as possible while the ball comes into contact with only the fingertips. The head should be up and eyes looking straight ahead. The player should move the ball around their waist as fast as possible, without losing control. Suggested repetitions: 50 times around each way x 2 *(or until you have become totally exhausted).*

Keep head up.

Move the ball as fast as you can.

Around the Knees:

Following the same process as the around the waist exercise, now the ball is moving rapidly around the knees. The circles should be tighter and the head should remain up.

Suggested repetitions: 50 times around each way x 2 *(or until failure)*

Always keep head up, never look down.

Around the Ankles:

Moving now below the knees down to the ankles and following the same pattern, making sure the circles are as tight as possible without hitting the ankles and going as fast as possible without losing control of the ball. Control is most easily kept if the ball only comes into contact with the fingertips.

Suggested repetitions: 50 times around each way x 2 *(or until failure)*

Single Ankle Wrap:

Similar to "Around the Ankles," the single ankle wrap should be the quickest exercise. Move the ball rapidly around one leg, as you go around the ankle you should be alternating hands. *(anywhere from the ankle to the knee).*

Suggested repetitions: 50 times around each way x 2 *(or until failure)*

Around the Head:

This is a bit more difficult as it is hard to ensure that the ball passes directly in front of the nose every time. The key to this drill is keeping the head stationary.

Suggested repetitions: 50 times around each way x 2 *(or until failure)*

Ball Squeeze "Hot Popper": The key to quick hands

This is one of the best ways to strengthen the fingers and improve ball control. The arms should be extended and above the head. The ball should rest on the fingertips and the player should squeeze their fingers together as fast as possible so that the ball is constantly being popped back out.

Suggested repetitions: 50 times x 2 *(or until failure)*

The ball will "pop" off finger tips.

This drill is great to build strength in the fingers.

Passing Figure Eight: (Ball should never touch the floor)

As the name implies, this involves the player moving the ball as quickly as possible between the legs and around in both directions. The key is to keep the lower body stationary as most of the movement will come from the arms, combined with limited movement in the torso.

Suggested repetitions: 25 times x 2 *(or until failure)*

Important Hint:
A. *Keep your head up.*
B. *Keep a solid, wide stance.*
C. *Move the ball as quickly as possible.*

High/Low Stationary Dribble:

Standing still with the left/right hand behind your back, dribble at normal height with the left/right hand and slowly dribble lower to the point where the ball barely bounces off the ground. Then slowly bring it back up to the normal dribbling height again. In the beginning, you should "stall" on the low dribbles a few times while testing the limits of how low you can go while still maintaining a dribble. It is important to keep contact with the ball limited to your fingertips to have maximum control.

Suggested repetitions: 10 times x 2 *(or until failure)*

Around the Leg:

Start with the left hand behind the back and the right hand on the ball. While keeping the head up, dribble around the right foot as fast as possible while keeping the dribbles low to the ground. Then alternate so that the left hand is dribbling the ball around the left foot while the right hand is behind the back.

Suggested repetitions: 25 times x 2 *(or until failure)*

This completes the basic ball handling skills section. Once a player feels comfortable with these, they are ready to move on to some of the more intermediate exercises.

Intermediate Ball Handling Drills

Dribbling Figure Eight:

As the name implies, this involves the player moving the ball as quickly as possible between the legs and around in both directions while dribbling. The technique is similar to the basic Figure Eight. The goal is to dribble as few times as possible, ensuring that the motion is fluid and quick. Remember to keep the head up! Alternatively, a player can dribble more frequently as they do the figure eight if they want to practice low dribbles.

Suggested repetitions: 25 times x 2

Pendulum Dribble: (Front to back)

Keeping the left arm behind the back and the left foot out in front (as if standing on a straight line) so that there is about 3-4 feet between the right and left leg. The right arm should be stretched out in front so that it is at the same angle as the left leg. Begin by bouncing the ball on the ground at such an angle so that the ball will come up and hit the right hand as it is full extended behind the player after making a "pendulum" type swing. Repeat same procedures with the left hand. Make sure the right leg is in front, and the right hand is behind the back.

Suggested repetitions: 25 times x 2

Straddle Dribble:

Stand on a straight line with the right or left foot in front and the legs spread apart (about 3-4 feet) so that the head is facing down the line (i.e. nose is parallel to the line). Keep the legs straight at the knee. Then bounce the ball from your right hand to your left hand with one quick dribble between the legs. The harder the ball bounces and the quicker one can bounce the ball between the legs, the better.

Suggested repetitions: 25 times x 2

Two-Hand Rocker:

Stand on a straight line with both feet on the line so that your nose is perpendicular to the line. (Keep the legs straight at the knee) Hold the ball with both hands out in front (arms extended) and bounce the ball between your legs and catch it as it bounces up behind you. Your hands should pass by your sides as you reach behind to catch the ball on the upward bounce. Then, without bringing the ball in front of you, quickly bounce the ball back between your legs so that you catch it in front of you.

Suggested repetitions: 25 times x 2

Cradle:

Begin by squatting with both feet perpendicular to the line and holding the ball between the knees. Then lightly toss the ball up and quickly move the hands behind the legs to catch the ball before it hits the ground. If you cannot catch the ball before it hits the ground, try letting it bounce once to get the feeling down before attempting to catch it before it hits.

Suggested repetitions: 25 times x 2

Waterfall:

Begin by holding the basketball with both hands behind the head above the neckline. Then release the ball so that it drops vertically. Quickly bring the hands down and behind the back to catch the ball before it hits the ground.

Suggested repetitions: 25 times

Up-and-Over:

Start with the ball in both hands with palms facing up, at stomach level. Then toss the ball up over the head and catch it behind the back with both hands. The higher you throw the ball, the better.

Suggested repetitions: 25 times

Two Hand Dribble: (Requires two basketballs)

Start dribbling each ball with both hands, maintaining synchronous dribbling for each ball. Once you are comfortable with each ball and your dribbling is synchronized, practice going from high dribbles to as low as you can go, while still maintaining a dribble. It is important to keep the dribbles synchronized. Then once you feel comfortable with this, alternate dribbles.

Suggested repetitions: 25 times *(going from high to low)*

Finger Dribble:

Sit on the playing surface or squat so that you are low to the ground. Then take the ball and dribble with each finger on each hand. This will improve the strength in your fingers.

Suggested repetitions: 25 times with each finger

Drills – Advanced

Spinning the ball on finger:

Often criticized for being a "useless" and "show-off" skill, the finger spin is a fun drill that you should have in your ball handling tool kit. By practicing this drill, you will gain further comfort with the basketball and improve ball control as you must focus intensely in order to keep the ball spinning. Once you have mastered this with one finger, you should be able to spin the ball on each finger of each hand. Then you should be able to switch between spinning it on the knuckles and the fingers without stopping. Finally you should attempt to spin it off your finger and bounce it onto the knee and catch it (while the ball is still spinning) with the finger.

How to Spin the Ball

A. Hold the ball with two hands, one in the front, and one behind the ball.

B. Quickly snap your hands in the same direction and lightly toss the ball in the air.

C. Slide your right index finger under the ball while the ball is spinning.

D. Find the "sweet spot" directly under the ball.

Diagonal Cradle:

Assume the same starting position as the cradle, but hold the ball so that one arm is behind the leg and the other arm is in front of the other leg. The ball should be resting in the hands about 1.5 feet off the ground and between the knees. Then lightly toss the ball up and quickly move the hands so that they are opposite positions and catch the ball before it hits the ground. If you cannot catch the ball before it hits the ground, try letting it bounce once to get the feeling down before attempting to catch it before it hits.

Suggested repetitions: 25 times x 2

Spider Dribble:

Start with both hands holding the ball about 1 foot off the ground and between the knees. The starting position should look similar to the cradle. Then dribble it so that the right hand does the first dribble in front and then the left hand dribbles the next in front. While the left hand is dribbling the right hand should move behind the knees and dribble it after the left hand has dribbled in front. Then the left hand moves behind the knee and dribbles it back after the right hand has done so. The ball should remain in relatively the same position, but the hands should be alternating from front to back in a very rapid motion.

Suggested repetitions: 25 times x 2

Two Hand Running Dribble: (Requires two basketballs)

Start dribbling each ball with both hands, maintaining synchronous dribbling for each ball. *(Same starting position as the intermediate Two Hand Dribble).* Once you are comfortable with each ball and your dribbling is synchronized, start running up and down the court with both balls bouncing at your sides. Alter the height of the dribbles as you go. Once you can get into a full out sprint while keeping both balls in a synchronized bounce, try alternating dribbles so that when one hits the ground, the other touches your hand.

Note: When reaching the other end of the court, you can make a "U-turn" with the balls, or just leave the balls bouncing while you turn your body around.

Suggested repetitions: 10 roundtrip sprints up and down the court

Running Cradle:

To gain comfort with this, begin with the ball between your legs with one foot in front of the other. Hold the ball about 1.0 – 1.5 feet off the ground. Take a step forward so that you are forced to move the ball in to the opposite hand and with each step you will put the ball through the legs and into the opposite hand. Try walking up and down the court while doing this the first few times. As you get better, you should be able to run *(while hunched over, but with the head up)*

Suggested repetitions: 5 roundtrips up and down the court

Squat-Dribble:

Lean against the wall in the squat position while holding the ball. Then proceed to dribble under your legs from side to side as quickly as possible. Most coaches simply have their players squat against the wall to strengthen their leg muscles. This drill helps your ball handling co-ordination while also strengthening your leg muscles.

Suggested repetitions: 5 – 10 (1) minute intervals

Hail-Mary:

Throw the ball up in the air and catch it as it falls behind you. The trick is to catch the ball while you are bent over and your arms are extended out between your legs. How high you throw the ball is up to you

Shuffle-Dribble:

Similar to the straddle dribble, the shuffle dribble *(page 53)* is a bit more complicated as the player will take a step forward with each dribble between the legs. (It is recommended that you start with the ball in your right hand and bounce it through the legs while you are standing in the straddle position with the left foot forward). Passing the ball from left hand to right and right to left by bouncing it between the legs as you move forward will take some practice. Once you can walk all the way down the court and back without losing control of the ball, you can begin to add some tricks to the drill.

As you pass the ball between the legs with your hand (right), touch your left hand side waist, shoulder and ear before quickly getting your hand back into position to receive the next dribble. Do the same with the left hand immediately after passing the ball through the legs.

Suggested repetitions: 5 roundtrips up and down the court

Nutcracker:

This is essentially the same as the two hand rocker drill. However, you are not going to bounce the ball from your posterior side to the front side. The only bounce is a very hard one between the legs and a catch on the backside. How hard you throw the ball is up to you. Just be careful!!!

Suggested repetitions: Personal Choice

Chapter
FOUR

Dribbling & Spin Moves
LEARNING TO
TRASH THE DEFENSE

Dribbling

Practicing good dribbling skills is extremely important to the development of a solid ball-handler. Pay attention to detail and keep the ball on the fingertips.

Hand should never be under the ball.

The off-ball hand should be used to ward off the defense.

Start with the hand on the ball. The fingers on the hand should be spread out across the ball

The fingertips control the ball at all times and guide the direction the ball will take.

Never allow the hand to go under the ball during the dribble. This habit is very difficult to break. A lot of young players get the hand under the ball on a dribble and sometimes try to pass off the dribble. This is a very difficult pass to throw and to catch. The receiving player cannot pick up the flight of the pass quick enough and the ball tends to take off and sail making it very difficult to catch.

When dribbling, always protect the ball with your left hand or off-ball hand. This will keep the defense from getting too close and it actually helps with offensive balance.

Head is looking up for passing lanes and other offensive opportunities.

When attacking the basket using your dribble always have your head up and be studying the floor. Learning to dribble not looking down at the floor is difficult and it takes a lot of practice. But if you can dribble and read the floor you become a dangerous offensive threat.

Off hand protects ball.

This hand gives balance to the dribbler.

Notice how this player is protecting the ball, and keeps a keen eye on the offensive end of the court, looking for passing lanes and open shot opportunities.

The Basic Spin Moves

B

Place a chair between the free throw line and the basket. Start dribbling at the half court line and drive straight towards the chair.

As you approach the chair *(photo A)* keep the ball in your right hand, and use your left hand to protect the ball. Stop on the left foot, just to the right of the chair.

This right foot is too far out. This is the ideal spot.

A

(Photo A) Slide your right foot to the left and begin to pivot off your left foot. At this point you will change hands, and now begin to dribble with the left hand. It is extremely important to get your head around as quickly as possible. Keeping the head up and facing the basket.

The ideal spot to place your right foot *(photo C)* is just past the leg of the chair. Your right hand now protects the ball and you should be dribbling with your left hand. Your hips should be past the chair, and your shoulders should continue to turn to become square with the basket.

C

Foot should slip behind leg of chair.

D

E

(Photo D & E) Your have cleared the chair and now you should head directly to the basket. The key to executing a great spin move is to try to stay in a straight line to the basket.

You have now cleared the chair and should be heading to the basket.

Multiple Spin Moves

Take the next step

Learn to "pop" two or three spin moves going to the basket. Using chairs or other similar props you can simulate multiple defenders. Practice going both to the right and to the left.

Things you must do to be successful:

- Keep your drive to the basket tight and stay in a straight line.
- Keep the ball low and between your legs on the reverse dribble to prevent the defense from swiping it.
- Keep your head up and get it around to face the basket as quickly as possible on each spin move.
- Anticipate defenders jumping over to help.
- Be able to stop and pull up for the jump shot.

The offensive player should dribble right to the defensive player. Then at the last moment, the offensive player will start the spin.

The ► offensive players right foot will be planted and used as a pivot foot. The left foot begins to drop around behind the defense. The head should be looking up toward the defense. The offensive player will at this point change dribbling hands. Now the left hand will take over and push the ball between the offensive player's legs.

This foot will slide behind leg or chair.

Get head around facing basket.

◄ The left leg will reach around and step behind the defender's leg. The offensive player should keep the ball low and in between the legs.

66

Lead foot has to get behind defense. Foot should be close to chair.

As the offensive player steps around, the shoulders and head should pass by the defense.

This player right foot is too far away from chair.

The left leg now reaches out to step around the defense. Notice how the ball is being dribbled right between the player's legs away from the defense. The offensive player's head should be getting around and looking at the basket. This player is a little slow; his head should already be around facing the basket.

Don't be afraid to challenge the defense – get close, then spin.

Here the offensive player has gotten by one defender and is heading to the second. Again dribble as close to the defender as you can, then start the spin move.

The ball is being protected by player's body.

Again the player has spun around the defense and is keeping a straight line to the basket.

The Post Up Move

This move is dynamite!

If an offensive player can learn how to execute this move, he or she will have an advantage that is difficult to stop. A center, forward or guard can use this play.

A

Here the offensive player catches the ball and keeps both feet on the ground. This is critical to the success of this move.

B

The offensive player begins by reaching to the left, using the ball as "bait," while making the defense think that is the way he is going to drive. Notice how the offensive player's head and arms are reaching to the left.

C

Foot slips behind.

The defense will think you are going to the left by letting him see the ball and getting him to reach or get off balance. The offensive player's right foot is now slipping behind the defensive player.

D

Hints:
- Ball speed is a must
- Give a sharp head fake
- Tease defense with ball *(photo C)*

The offensive player quickly pivots to the right getting the hips and shoulder behind the defense.

F

The defense is behind and not a factor. The defense can only commit a foul at this point to stop the offensive player.

E

Here the offensive player is well past the defense. The offensive player will have a clear path to the basket. One quick dribble and this player is on the way to the basket.

Chapter
FIVE

How To
Play
DEFENSE

Defensive Balance

When playing defense it is important to maintain balance.

If you relate body position to that of a tightrope walker there is a strong relationship to balance and body position. The position of the hands and arms is critical for staying balanced. Having the hands pointing upwards and just outside the shoulders you have a perfect position for balance.

The bar used by tightrope walkers is used for balance. The palms of the hands need to point up so the grip on the bar is just outside the shoulders.

A basketball player needs the same balance when playing defense. The feet should be shoulder width apart, and the knees bent, having the back straight and palms up. The defensive player should focus their eyes directly on the center of the offensive player's chest. Never watch the movement of the ball.

Eyes focused on offensive players chest.

Palms pointing up.

Feet shoulder width apart.

This player has perfect defensive positioning. The palms are pointing up, the feet are shoulder width apart, and the eyes are focusing on the offensive player's chest. The palms pointing up allows the defensive player to reach and swipe at the ball in such a way as not to draw a foul.

Defensive Drop Step

The next skill in developing a strong defensive position is the Drop Step. The drop step allows a defensive player to contain an offensive player. The drop step helps the defensive player stay in front of the offensive player.

A

Nice wide stance.

B

Player is on "Balls of feet."

In this photo the defensive player is reacting to an offensive player moving to the right. The defensive player drops his left foot back, and slides over re-establishing his position in front of the offensive player. The left foot drops back at an angle cutting off the offensive player's movement to the basket.

C

Sliding over to get in front of offensive player.

D

Cutting off left handed dribbler.

Stopping An Offensive Player

A solid basketball player must develop defensive skills. One of the most important elements is the defensive drop step. A player who wishes to become very good should have this skill by the time they enter high school. This defensive move is used to contain and stop the offensive player.

A

Eyes on chest. Never watch the ball.

Notice how the feet are apart and player is on "Balls of feet."

B

Eyes on chest. Never watch the ball.

Hand in passing lane.

The left foot drops about two feet.

As the offensive player dribbles to the right, the defensive player drops the left foot back about two feet. The defensive player should try to keep his hand in the offensive player's passing lane.

Any time a defensive player gets in front of the ball handler, it is important to establish a stable defensive stance. Here the defensive player's feet are shoulder width apart and his hands are facing up. The head is focused on the ball handler's chest and the back is straight. Knees should be slightly bent.

C

Eyes on chest. Never watch the ball.

The defensive player then slides over in front of the offensive ball handler. This has to be a quick and smooth slide. The defense then re-establishes his position in front of the ball handler.

Defensive player is back in front of the ball hander.

D

Same step but to the left.

As the offensive ball handler switches to the left hand and tries to dribble, the defense drops the right foot and slides over in front. The same move on defense that was used to go to the left is now used on the right side.

73

Slide & Glide

Playing defense with the feet

The feet are the most important part of playing defense. It is very important to keep the feet sliding across the floor.

Never allow your feet to cross.

It is important to have a solid open stance, with the palms facing up and the feet shoulder width apart. When you drop step to the side to cut off the offensive player, it is equally important to slide back in front of the offensive player making the offensive player change directions or pick up the dribble. A good defensive player should always be about two feet back and in front of the offense. If you get too close, the offense will drive around you or you will get called for a foul.

These two photos show how not to play defense. This player is crossing his feet and is off balance.

This photo shows the defense picking up the right foot too far off the floor. This takes time and allows the offense to dribble around the defensive player.

The feet should never be off the floor more than 2 inches.

WRONG

This player is sliding to the left dropping the right foot, staying low and moving to cut off the dribble. The player is gliding or moving on the balls of the feet, off the heals. Hands are facing upward.

Chapter SIX

Big Time Basketball SKILLS

HOW TO Set A Screen

Learning this skill is sometimes very difficult, especially for a young developing player. Most beginning or young players shy away from the contact that is necessary to set a solid screen.

This player is setting a solid screen by taking a wide stance and using his elbows to contain the defensive player.

The offensive player for whom the screen has been set must also do his or her part to ensure the success of the screen. As they drive to the right they must come as close to the teammate setting the screen as they can. This will keep the defensive player from slipping through the screen.

Offensive player should dribble as close as possible to the person setting the screen.

After a screen has been set, the person who set the screen becomes the "Roller". Here the screen is set, and the offensive player on the right begins to roll or pivot towards the basket. The left hand or hand closest to the ball handler opens up and leads the beginning of the "roll".

Roller giving a target for the pass.

The offensive player should hold off the person he just set the screen against.

The offensive players right foot is the pivot foot. The offensive player's stomach should face the ball handler all the time.

Notice the player rolling to the basket, has his stomach facing the ball, and the left hand open as a target for a pass.

Here the offensive player has completed the turn and is heading to the basket ready to receive the pass from the dribbler.

HOW TO Box Out An Offensive Player After A Shot

It is very important to know how to execute this skill. Most coaches expect their players to be able to box out. Becoming good at this requires a lot of practice. An effective box-out can allow a team to gain a big advantage over the competition. Teams that display strong box out capabilities will usually limit other teams to one shot at each possession.

The offensive player is about to shoot the ball. The defensive player is putting a hand in the shooters vision, and beginning to pivot towards the shooter.

The right foot of the defensive player should step to the outside of the shooters right foot. The defensives players right hand and arm should come under the shooters shooting arm.

The defensive player brings his left foot back and his hips up against the shooters waist. The defensive players elbows and hands will act as a barrier to hold the shooter back. The hips and backside are used to hold the shooter back. The defensive player will continue to hold the shooter off the until he sees the direction of the rebound and then go to retrieve the ball.

Hands in the air to aviod getting called for a foul.

You can hold a player using this part or your backside.

Getting A Rebound

And setting up for the outlet pass

When you pull a rebound off the defensive end of the court it is important to grab the ball with both hands. Never bring the ball down anywhere near your waist, keep the ball high around the shoulders and begin to turn toward to the right or left. Get your head around as fast as possible. Looking for your teammates, you should begin to pivot and turn toward your end of the court.

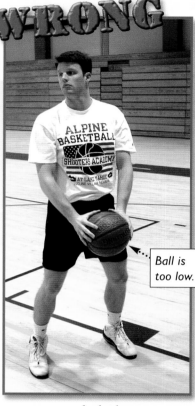

WRONG

Ball is too low.

Pulling a rebound off the defensive boards, hands are grabbing the ball, feet are square to the basket.

The ball is high, and the player begins his turn towards the offensive end of the court.

Getting the head around and finding a teammate for the outlet pass. Notice the right foot is the pivot foot.

The player looks down the court to get a clear vision of where the pass is going to be thrown. The over head pass is the most effective, and best pass to throw for the outlet pass.

Offensive Rebound & Put Back

When getting an offensive rebound it is important to keep the ball high. Learn to shoot immediately. Practice by throwing the ball against the backboard. Go up and grab the ball, keeping the ball high as you return to the floor. Quickly jump and shoot. Never bring the ball down below your shoulders. This skill is difficult because it takes timing and rhythm while shooting.

WRONG

Never bring the ball down on a rebound

If you bring the ball down, the defensive players will grab the ball before you have a chance to shoot. Or the ball will get knocked out of your hands. Bringing the ball down takes time and allows the defense to react.

Always Face Up To Basket

When You Catch a Pass

Whenever you receive a pass it is a must to always pivot and face the basket.

When you "Face Up" you open up the following options:

- *You see your teammates for possible passes.*
- *You may have an open shot.*
- *You may be able to drive to the basket.*

In this photo the player has caught the pass and is beginning to pivot toward the basket.

This player is making sure to protect the ball from the defensive player, keeping it out of the defensive players reach.

This player decided to take the open shot after "Facing Up" to the basket.

- - - - - - - - - - - - - - - - - - -

If you don't "Face Up":

- *You will not see your teammates*
- *The defensive player gains the advantage; it will give the defense more time to get in position.*
- *You will miss many opportunities to pass.*

Working To Develop Lively Feet

The feet are extremely critical to developing an accurate shot. Having "**lively feet**" will lead to a sound and accurate shot. The feet must be square to the basket before the shot is released. Once the feet are set the shoulders and hips will also be set and ready to complete the shot. As a player moves to get into position to shoot the first thing to get into line are the feet. Most players do not pay attention to feet position prior to the shot. If the feet are square the shot percentages will improve drastically.

Drills to develop lively feet:

Player's hand begins to ask for ball.

Left shooting elbow.

Elbow to elbow, with a pivot:

Work the feet and develop strong coordination between the upper body and the lower body. It is extremely important to practice shooting by changing positions on the floor after each shot. The pivot allows you to develop lively feet and precise coordination with the shot.

After a shot has been released the shooter begins the pivot. The player starts the pivot by dropping the right foot back and turning the shoulders. The left foot is used as the pivot point. It is important that the shooter's head completes a 360° degree turn as fast as possible. The player's eyes should make contact with the basket. This will force the player to get the body around and heading toward the basket.

3

After the player has completed the shot on the left side, he reverses and returns to the right side of the court. A player should shoot at least 25 of these shots. A pivot should be used from each side. Players should record the number of shots made.

5

As the player reaches the opposite side of the floor it is very important to bring the body and feet around so they are square to the basket. If a player fails to do this, they will have a much lower shooting percentage.

As the player reaches the opposite side of the floor the inside foot or the right foot is the pivot foot, and the left foot is used to balance and turn the body. It is very important to get the shoulder square to the basket before taking the shot.

4

6

Right shooting elbow.

This player has completed the turn back to the basket. The feet are square and the shoulders have come around square to the basket. Right handed players going to the left always have a problem getting the shoulders and feet square to the basket. *(See page 21 for a complete explanation of this problem).*

Chapter SEVEN

Developing A SOLID WORK ETHIC

Developing A Solid Work Ethic

To become a great basketball player you must have a solid individual workout plan.

This plan should include specific daily drills. These drills should be designed to improve the skills needed to play competitive basketball.

Very few players have any kind of planned workout schedule where they allocate time each day to perfect their individual basketball skills. The player who develops a plan and sticks to the workout schedule will have a tremendous advantage over those players who have unplanned workouts. Most basketball players usually spend time practicing skills they have mastered. Generally young developing players do not spend enough time working on new skills. Difficult skills are often never learned.

This is the point where great players distinguish themselves.

In this chapter, simple work out program can be modified to fit the needs of any player. It is a foundation that becomes a player's daily schedule. Following a plan will give a player a clear understanding of how to develop outstanding basketball skills.

To decide which skills to work on check the player *(skill list on page 92)* to see what needs to be added to your schedule. Learned skills need to be practiced as well as skills still in the developmental stages. Try to practice and work to improve your skills each and every day. Finding time to practice is difficult. A student athlete must balance his or her educational goals with athletic goals. If you develop a realistic schedule and discipline yourself, you will have time to reach your potential for both goals.

A basketball player has three distinct practice seasons:

1. *The off-season*
2. *The game season*
3. *The summer season*

SAMPLE WORK OUT SCHEDULES

1. The "Off-season" workout schedule:

From the end of a basketball season to the beginning of summer.

Weekday schedule

Before school:
(Times will vary depending on school schedule)

7:00 a.m. to 8:00 a.m.
  Shooting
- Shot check: zone 1: *100 shots – 10 minutes*
- Elbow to elbow Zone 3: *100 shots – 10 minutes*
- Elbow to elbow Zone 5: *100 shots – 10 minutes*

  Spin moves to the left: *15 minutes*
  Spin moves to the right: *15 minutes*
  Eat large breakfast

8:30 a.m. to 12:00 p.m.
  Attend Classes

Lunch: *12:00 p.m. to 12:45 p.m.*
(If you have a place on campus where you could make this a working lunch, shoot and eat)

12:45 p.m. to 3:00 p.m.
  Attend Classes

After school work-out session:

3:30 p.m. to 5:00 p.m.
  Dribbling, Shooting, passing, Lay-ups Speed dribbles, Spin moves

5:30 p.m. to 6:30 p.m.
  Dinner

After dinner workout:

6:30 p.m. to 7:30 p.m.
  Shooting drills

7:30 p.m. to 10:30 p.m.
  Work on school assignments

Weekend Schedule

Saturday and Sunday:

10:00 a.m. to 12:00 noon
  Shot check: *(500 shots where each shot is analyzed and refined)*
  Elbow to elbow Shooting drills – Zones 2-3-4-5

Ball speed: *Use dumbbell to develop quick ball speed movement (page 100)*

Passing: Work on all types of passes either with another player or throw at a target placed on a wall.

Dribbling: Around chairs, trash cans, or cones in a parking lot.

Lunch: *12:00 p.m. to 1:00 p.m.*

1:00 p.m. to 4:00 p.m.

Other activities other than basketball such as school assignments etc.

4:00 p.m. to 6:00 p.m.

Practice

Spin moves: *(place trashcans, or chairs and practice spin moves page 65)*

Full court game: *(use all the skills needed to play a full court game)*

Shot check: *(work to make sure everything is in line before you move back away from the basket to begin to practice shooting)*

Super 100: *(Non stop 100 shots in a row, moving across the key in zones 3,4,5,6. Using a pivot after each shot.*

2. Summer workout schedule:

This is the best time to develop as a basketball player. Distractions, school responsibilities and homework will not interfere with basketball practice. This is a time to work on all those skills that will make a complete player. One skill, which should be a major part of the summer plan, is the development of a player's shot. Shooting up to 2000 shots per day will guarantee that you are a "Pure Shooter" in the fall.

Summer Team or Club basketball:

(It is important that you have an option to play summer team basketball. Either through a school team or a club team there is a chance to try skills in a less pressured environment. Some players will compete on two different summer league teams. The more a player is exposed to real game situations, the greater his or her understanding is of the basketball skills needed to compete at the highest level).

9:00 a.m. to 12:00 p.m.

Shooting workout

Shot check: *300*

Zone one elbow to elbow: *(500)*

Zone two elbow to elbow: *(300)*

Zone four elbow to elbow: *(300)*

Full court dribble drills:

Change of speed and direction: *(Ball Handling)*

Pivot dills

Passing drills: *(pages 41-51)*

3. The Basketball Game Season workout schedule:

7:00 a.m. to 8:00 p.m.
   Shooting workout: *(see page 37)*

8:00 a.m. to 12:00 p.m.
   Attend classes

12:00 p.m. to 12:45 a.m.
   Lunch shooting workout

12:45 p.m. to 3:00 p.m.
   Attend classes

3:00 p.m. to 5:00 p.m.
   Attend School Basketball practice

5:00 p.m. to 6:30 p.m.
   Complete Homework and dinner

6:30 p.m. to 7:30 p.m.
   Dribble, ball handling, or shooting drills *(on your own – aside from organized team practice)*

7:30 p.m. to 9:00 p.m.
   Complete Homework

Weekend Schedule

8:00 a.m. to 12:00 p.m.
   Same as the summer schedule

2 Hours
   Team practice

Practice hints:
(Things your competition doesn't practice).

- Practice tired.
- Spend time to perfect all. Work on problem areas *(i.e. weak side dribbling)*.
- Stay focused.
- Don't quit when tired.
- Don't get frustrated – if your are not having fun, don't force it.
- Don't get mad, get even.
- The extra time you spend is time your competition is not spending.
- Practice wisely.
- You can pay now or you can complain later.
- Finding time to practice takes effort. Making excuses is effortless.
- A star is not born; a star is developed through dedicated work ethics.

Rules Of The Game

- When you catch the ball always face up to the basket.
- Never bring the ball down on a rebound.
- Always come to meet the ball when it is being passed to you.
- Always pass ahead, never to a player directly in front or behind you. Use the angle.
- Never chase a player with the ball by running along side, cut the player off and slow down the ball.
- If you do not have the ball you should be setting yourself up for a pass or rebound. Use off the ball movement.
- Never dribble unless you are going toward the basket; taking one dribble and stopping is never allowed. Never stop your dribble just across half court; go to the top of the key.
- Never take off without a flight plan. Know what you are going to do before you leave your feet.
- Never give up the baseline.

Things You Need to Learn to be a Successful Basketball Player

- How to shoot correctly.
- How to pass.
- How to pivot, both on offense and defense.
- Be able to think and play.
- Know how to set a solid and effective screen.
- Understand how to go from offense to defense.
- Be able to see the floor.
- Know how to box out.
- When you go into the game know whom you will be assigned to guard, and your role in the offense and defense.

Words To Live By For A Complete Basketball Player

Never accept a missed shot:
Carefully analyze each missed shot attempt. Look to see where the ball hit and fix the problem before the next shot. Each shot you take will be a guide for next shot.

You CANNOT stop a shooter:
A defensive player cannot stop an offensive player who knows how to shoot. Through the effective use of ball-speed and footwork, any offensive player can "out-smart" any defensive player.

Attention to detail:
Make sure you practice correct fundamentals and work toward eliminating bad habits.

If you are standing still, you are doing something wrong:
A great basketball player should be constantly moving and identifying opportunities on the court. On the offensive end, a player should work toward getting open for a shot via "off-the-ball" movements. When not looking for a scoring opportunity, a player should be an integral part of his/her team's offense (*i.e. setting an effective pick, creating a passing lane or getting in position for a rebound*). On the defensive end, a player should always look for ways to become an offensive player (*i.e. looking for a steal, forcing the defense to take a bad shot, boxing out another player*).

If you find yourself standing still or "flat-footed" at either end of the court, you are doing something wrong!

Gym time is work time:
When you walk into a gym, you must be mentally prepared to begin work. Utilize your time effectively. If you are not using your time effectively, it is guaranteed that somebody else is and when you meet him or her in competition one day, they will have the upper hand.

When you are tired, you are ready to learn:
The best time to learn is when you are fatigued or exhausted. A player must learn to "practice tired." When fatigued, one's capacity to pay attention to detail and concentrate is diminished. Many players get tired and go home. It is the great players who overcome fatigue and work harder to correct problems. Practicing tired will also provide a player with the experience to come through in the crucial 4th quarter/overtime period.

Always have a "Flight Plan":
When you leave your feet, know where you are going to land. Many players will jump or take off before they know where they are going. Coaches refer to this as "being out of control." The end result leads to either an offensive foul for charging or a turnover.

Never show emotion on the court:
When playing in a game do not allow your emotions to show. Always play under control. It is a lot easier said than done, but a player who is a master of their emotions will never lose control. If you display emotion, you will lose both your focus on the game and your ability to showcase your talents.

Play through your mistakes:

If you make a mistake on the court, don't make a big deal out of it, as your display of frustration will only magnify the mistake. Most coaches will replace a player who makes a mistake and then shows added emotion. Simply forget the mistake and continue playing. This will help to minimize the mistake and people will forget about it. Great players get over their mistakes and learn from them.

Let your talent do the talking:

Concentrate on the things you need to do while playing. Be aware of everything that is taking place in the game. Never talk to the other team. Let your skills and talent speak for you. Always show poise and confidence.

Work towards perfection:

When practicing, always strive to do everything correctly. Never accept a mistake and work diligently to perfect each and every fundamental.

Never shoot from the "no-shot zone":

The no shot zone is the area located behind the basket and extends to the baseline corners. *(See Shooting Zones on page 19)*. Taking a shot from this area will lower your shooting percentage. It is very difficult to make baskets from the "No Shot Zone". Taking one step towards the middle of the court will increase your chances of making a basket by 40 percent.

Deliver the mail:

When you have the ball in your possession make sure you take care of it. Getting the ball to a teammate is critical and the player who is passing the ball is responsible for ensuring that the pass can successfully be completed. This process is referred to as "delivering the mail." If you don't take care of the ball you won't see much playing time. Driving the length of the court and missing an open lay-up would be considered a prime example of "not delivering the mail."

Always release pressure:

Pressure is created when a defensive player "over plays" or "smothers" an offensive player in possession of the ball. The offensive player must "release" the pressure by either driving to the basket or passing the ball to a teammate. This is a MUST to keep the defense from gaining an advantage or intimidating an offensive player.

If you play with your head down, you are going down:

Keep your head up at all times. See the entire floor. Keeping your head up allows you to see passing lanes and assess offensive opportunities.

If you haven't felt failure, success won't mean much:

Success only comes after failure. If you work to correct mistakes, you will be successful. Never give up!

Player Skills Checklist

This checklist is a simple way to follow a basketball player development. This checklist should be reviewed regularly.

OFFENSIVE SKILLS

Shooting:

Check off for each shooting zone. Shoot 100 shots from each zone and check when you have reached each level. These shots should be off a pivot, going elbow to elbow without stopping. List your percentages and watch your improvement. When you reach the expected levels you will be considered a "PURE SHOOTER."

_____ **Zone One:** Can make 96 out of 100 shots.

_____ **Zone Two:** Can make 92 out of 100 shots.

_____ **Zone Three:** Can make 85 out of 100 shots.

_____ **Zone Four:** Can make 80 out of 100 shots.

_____ **Zone Five:** Can make 75 out of 100 shots.

_____ **Zone Six**: Can make 70 out of 100 shots.

_____ **Zone Seven:** can make 65 out of 100 shots.

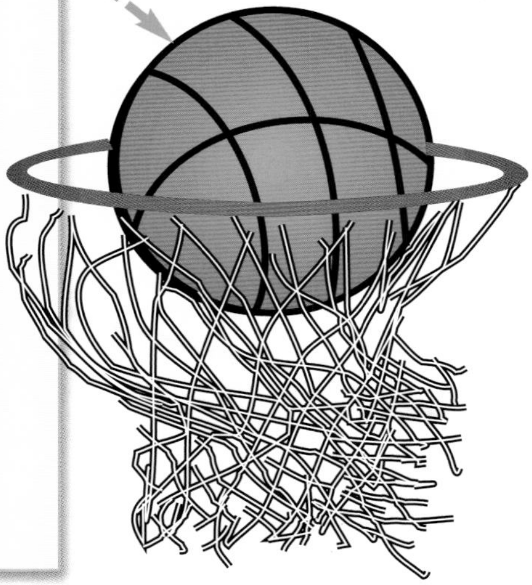

Individual Rating Scale:
CHECK MONTHLY TO SEE IF YOU HAVE IMPROVED

10 Player has mastered skill.

9 Player can use skill to some degree, but needs more practice.

8 Player has limited use of this skill; player needs lots of practice to be able to use this skill.

7 Player has not developed this skill and should not use in a game situation.

6 Player has very limited use of this skill and needs practice to use this skill.

5 Player does not have this skill.

Passing:

The following skills should be rated on a scale of 10 to 5.

_____ Ball speed. *(See pages 99-101 for details).*

_____ Passing above the shoulders.

_____ Left handed pass.

_____ Right handed pass.

_____ Right handed bounce pass.

_____ Left handed bounce pass.

Off Ball Movement:

This measures a player's ability to move without the ball, creating open shots.

_____ Ability to set screens *(pick)*.

_____ Ability to use a screen *(pick and roll)*.

_____ Ability to bounce and spin off other players.

_____ Ability to read the floor.

Dribbling:

_____ Left handed dribble, full speed never looking down.

_____ Right handed dribble, full speed never looking down.

_____ Left handed stop and go full speed, never looking down.

_____ Right handed dribble stop and go never looking down.

_____ Spin dribble, left.

_____ Spin dribble, right.

_____ Mutiple spin dribbles, alternating right and left hand, never looking down.

DEFENSIVE SKILLS

_____ Defensive position.

_____ Ability to cut off baseline.

_____ Ability to box out.

_____ Man to man defense, ability to stop very a good offensive player.

_____ Ability to read different defenses.

_____ Zone defense skills.

_____ Man to man skills.

TEAM SKILLS

_____ Ability to run offense and know your role.

_____ Ability to see passing lanes.

Things You Have To Learn To Be Successful

- How to shoot correctly; if you don't work at it someone else will.
- How to pass. Pass to open players coming toward you.
- How to pivot, both on offense and defense.
- Know your spot and place in the offense and defense.
- Be able to think and play.
- How to set a solid and effective screen, and to pivot off after you have set the screen.
- Understand how to go from offense to defense.
- Know how to play solid defense.
- Know where your spot is on inbounds plays.
- Be able to see the floor.
- Box out; get the rebound.
- When you go into the game, know whom you will be guarding and your role in offense and defense.

Chapter EIGHT

BUILDING THE RIGHT BODY

A Training Program For The Ultimate Basketball Player

The Anatomy
Of A Basketball Player . . .

Note: The weight training program on pages 98 to 105 will help you build strength in these muscle groups.

Having a solid weight training program will add strength to your total game.

Triceps

This is the "shot muscle" located in the bottom of the upper arm this muscle works the whole arm movement. It attaches to the shoulder blade, the backside of the upper arm and to the elbow. This muscle lifts the wrist and hand to get it into the proper position to shoot. Having well developed triceps will help you keep the ball above your head and out in front of your forehead during the shot.

Pectorals

Pectoralis major, the chest muscles. Very important in all upper arm movement. Passing, shooting and defensive skills all rely on the "pecs."

Upper Abdominal

Upper abdominals are located just below the rib cage. This muscle group controls all upper body strength. Rebounding, shooting and passing rely on these muscles.

Lower abdominal

Lower abdominals are located just below the stomach. This muscle group works the lower torso, and is extremely important in pivots, and spin moves.

Rectus Femoris

This muscle is located on the front of the upper leg and is used to extend the leg from a bent position. This is the most important muscle to gain speed in running, to get height in jumping and to get in position on rebounds. This muscle is really made up of four separate muscles which all come together at the kneecap.

Building A Strong Body

Latissimus Dorsi

These are the large muscles in the players back. These muscles are used for ball-speed and any over hand and shoulder movement. They help to get a basketball player's arms and shoulders square to the basket.

Gluteus Maximus

The gluteus maximus "the butt muscle" This is the largest muscle in the body. This muscle will help to rotate the thigh. Located right behind the hip joint this muscle is the "action muscle used to get the legs moving during a shot, spin moves, and acceleration on jump shots.

Gastrocnemius

This muscle helps to bend the knee and flex the foot downward. This muscle is very important in pivots, and jumping. Developing a strong gastrocnemius muscle a basketball player can increase his or her jumping ability.

Biceps Femoris

(The back thigh muscle) used to extend the hips, rotate the leg and flex the knee. This is a three-part muscle. Starting around the pelvis, and one reaches to the outer thigh and the other two go to the inner knee. This gives a basketball player "spring." It is a fragile and dangerous muscle to injure. By training and building strength and tone in this muscle a basketball player can add tremendous speed and jumping ability.

Trapezius

The trapezius muscle is the shoulder shrugging muscle, used to keep the head and shoulders in line during a shot. The trapezius muscle supports the shoulder blade when the shooting arm is raised above the head.

Deltoid

(shoulder muscle) Probably the most important muscle in the execution of the shot. This muscle lifts the arms and hands to place them in the proper shooting position. This muscle attaches itself to the shoulder blade and collarbone. It also is attached to the bone on the upper arm.

Soleus

This muscle flexes the foot downward. It has no involvement in the movement of the knee but it does help to drive the foot, jumpshot, and layups.

Weight Training Program For Basketball Players

NEVER USE MORE WEIGHT THAN YOU CAN HANDLE – "PRACTICE SAFE"

This is a program that is inexpensive and extremely productive.

The weight training exercises will help any basketball player achieve added strength as well as jumping ability. Upper body strength is extremely important for all basketball players. It is not recommended for players under the age of 12 to get too serious about lifting weights. Their bodies are still developing and they usually do more harm than good with an aggressive weight training program. Light weights are recommended for younger players. The following program, if followed, will add strength and jumping ability.

Basic Military Push-Up

Toes together, back straight, hands shoulder width apart. Three sets of twenty five.

Arm Chair Squat

Using a chair place both hands on the edge of the chair, legs out in front and then slowly lower to the ground. 3 sets of 10. Great for the triceps and chest muscles.

Ball-Speed With 8 Pound Medicine Ball

Using a weighted ball about the size of a regular basketball a player can to improve his or her passing and offensive skills. By using this heavy ball a player can develop incredible "ball speed." This skill gives offensive players many chances to get open.

Keep ball high and away from body.

Pivot foot.

Start with the weighted ball above your head keeping your feet shoulder width apart. Move the ball from side to side, never allowing the ball to drop below the shoulders.

Step two:

Same drill as above, but now incorporate a step and a pivot. Move the ball from side to side and reach and stretch, simulating passing techniques. *(See passing drills on page 42-45)*

Move the ball quickly – from point to point as you step.

Taking a long stride will help you develop solid balance.

DumbBell Ball-Speed Drill

Using a dumb-bell you can simulate ball-speed. Moving the dumb-bell from side to side and stepping to the right and left a player can develop unique skills with the basketball. This drill will help an offensive ball handler maintain balance. The faster you move the dumb-bell from right to left and back, the more dynamic the offensive move will be with a basketball.

Pivot foot.

Pivot foot.

Keep the DumbBell High.

Step and pivot as you "pump" the DumbBell.

Stay on the "balls of the feet."

Ball-Speed With A Basketball

After you use the 8-pound medicine ball and the dumbbell you will find doing ball-speed with a basketball very easy. And your quickness, speed and flexibility with the ball to be much improved. If a player uses all three (the medicine ball, the dumbbell and the basketball) any player will become extremely good at passing and getting open for a shot.

Practice quick snaps with the ball.

Keeping the ball high, it is difficult for the defense. If the defense gets too close, you drive; if the defense stays back, you shoot.

Keep the ball above the shoulders.

It is important to reach and snap the ball from side to side both with a pivot and with the feet shoulder width apart.

Bench Press
From a sitting position

Use a fairly light amount of weight. Feet flat on the ground, and go for it.

The Arm Curl

Using a bar bell with about 50 pounds, stand with your feet about shoulder width apart. Your hands should be upright and your back straight. Start with the bar down, and bring your hands to your chest. Do this slowly without jerking the bar. Start out with 10 curls, and rest, and repeat three times.

The Finger Roller

Use a barbell with about thirty pounds and allow the bar to roll from your palms to the tips of your fingers. When the bar reaches the fingertips curl the fingers around the bar and bring the fingers towards your chest, using your wrist to curl the bar towards you. Repeat this exercise 10 times rest and do three more sets. As you get stronger you may want to add weight to the bar. This in a must exercise for all shooting skills. The wrist and fingertips benefit the most from this exercise and they are the most crucial part of a players shot.

As the bar rolls downward, go slow for best results.

Let the bar roll to your finger tips.

Barbell Lunges

With a barbell located behind your head and resting on your shoulders alternate feet and step forwards and bend down as far as you can. Step back and use the other foot. Continue by doing at least 25, rest and repeat. Add weight when needed. This will strengthen your hamstring, and the calf, and thigh muscles.

DumbBell Arm Drop

Standing with your feet shoulders width apart, grab a dumbbell and raise the dumbbell behind the head. Drop the dumbbell straight down to the top of the shoulders. Start with a light weight that is easy to maneuver and add weight as you develop strength. This exercise is great for developing the biceps and triceps and shoulders muscles.

DumbBell Arm Curl

Sit in a chair, rest your elbow on your inner thigh.

Bring the dumbbell up to your chest slowly.

Allow the dumbbell to drop very slow.

Squats

With the barbell located behind the head and resting on the shoulders, bend the knees and squat. Keeping the back straight. The weight of the barbell should be directly over the feet. Your weight should be over the toes. This is great for the thighs, buttocks, and knee muscles. Start with small amount of weight and work up to larger weights.

The Toe Rise

This is great for developing the calf muscle. Players who wish to to increase their jumping ability can do it very quickly with this drill. Place a barbell on the shoulder with about 100 lbs or weight you can easily handle. Go to a curb, or place a 2 x 4 under your toes.

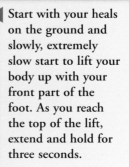

Start with your heals on the ground and slowly, extremely slow start to lift your body up with your front part of the foot. As you reach the top of the lift, extend and hold for three seconds.

The "Pigeon Lift" by turning your toes to the inside you will increase the difficulty of this drill. It will really help strengthen the ankles.

Glossary Of Terms

Active Feet: Ability to keep feet active, alert and responsive. A player must stay on the "balls" of their feet and not rest too much on their heels in order to quickly move from point-to-point.
(See "Balls of Feet" Photo)

Agility: The ability to move with a quick and easy grace. Being able to quickly adapt to changing defensive strategies and playing conditions. A successful player should be able to demonstrate his/her agility on the court in any situation.

Attitude: A player's perception of his/herself and others both on and off the court. Without question, this is the most important factor determining a player's success.

Ball-fake: A player using the ball to force a defensive player off balance. Using quick pump fakes to the left and right will make the defense react by leaning.

Ball-Speed: The ability of an offensive player to use the ball to force a defensive player to lose balance. Quick and precise movement of the basketball can create offensive opportunities.

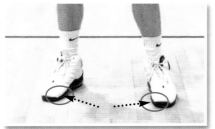

Balls-of-Feet: Area of foot that is right behind the toes. Best part of foot to help maintain balance.

Baseline: This is the line going underneath the basket and that marks the out of bounds. "Giving up the baseline" refers to an offensive player getting around a defensive player and going to the basket by way of the baseline.

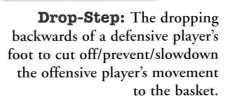

Baseline.

Box out: A defensive or offensive player keeping an opposing player from getting a rebound by using their body as a shield.

Bucket: Another common name for basket or hoop.

Coffin Corner: This is the area located at half court, where the half court line meets the sideline. If an offensive player crosses the half court line and stops dribbling they are stuck in the Coffin corner. Alternatively, this corner can be at the intersection of the baseline and sideline.

Crossover dribble: A dribble starting on either the right or left side of an offensive player. The player then switches to the other hand, dribbling in across and in front, the ball ends up on the opposite side of the player. Used to change directions when dribbling.

Double-dribble: A violation of the rules. When a player interrupts dribbling by touching the ball with both hands or "carrying" the ball between successive dribbles.

Defensive Balance: Defensive position, having both feet and hands in balance. Palms up and feet about shoulder width apart.

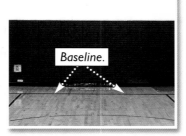

Drop-Step: The dropping backwards of a defensive player's foot to cut off/prevent/slowdown the offensive player's movement to the basket.

Defensive Position: A basketball player playing man-to-man defense on an offensive player. Maintaining a solid stance, and being on balance.

Elbow to Elbow:
This refers to the corners, which are made from the lines from the free-throw line to the line on the side of the key. From one edge of the free-throw line to the other.

Ear Pass: An offensive player making a pass right directly by past the ear of the defensive player. If done correctly, the defensive player will not have time to react to block the pass.

Face up: When a player gets into positions, he/she should be "square" with the basket when in possession of the ball. In order to see the floor and size up all available offensive opportunities, a player must be looking facing at the basket. This must be done as quickly as possible.

Fast break: The quick process of the offensive team moving the ball from the defensive end of the court to the offensive end. This transition is executed rapidly, usually through crisp passes to other offensive players further downcourt. This creates opportunities for scoring baskets. A well-executed fast break will result in an offensive advantage, as the defense does not have time to react and a fast break should lead to an easy bucket.

Flight plan: An offensive player's route to the basket. The decision to attack the basket and "go to the hole" should not be done without the player having thought about a route. Leaving one's feet and going airborne should not be done in uncertain circumstances. A confident and composed flight plan will prevent a player not turning the ball over or committing an offensive foul in the process. An offensive player with a good flight plan will be able to score when they leave the ground and head directly toward the basket.

Flat-Feet (Flat-Footed): When a player is standing on their heels. This makes them unable to respond or react quickly. A player should avoid getting "caught flat-footed."

Follow-through: When a shooter's hand, wrist and finger-tips continue towards the basket after releasing the basketball. A good follow-through is imperative to the successful completion of a basketball shot.

Help hand: The hand which is not shooting. The hand that supports the ball and the hand, which keeps the ball steady during a basketball shot. The proper position for the help hand is located on the side of the ball during the shot.

Half court line: The line, which separates the basketball court in two parts. Once an offensive player crosses this line (from the defensive side) they cannot go back. The term used to describe the area behind the half-court line is the "backcourt."

Jump Shot: When a player leaves the ground using timing, rhythm, and rotation to shoot.

Key (a.k.a. "the Lane" or "the Paint"): The area located under the basket upto the free throw line. This area is usually painted a solid color. An offensive player is only allowed to stay in this area for three seconds. They can return but only for three additional seconds. Failure to "clear the lane" (a.k.a. "camping out in the key") results in the loss of the ball. This is a violation because it gives the offense an unfair advantage if the post |players are trying to establish positions for too long. The violation only pertains to offensive players who do not have the ball in their hands while in the key.

Lively Feet: The state or condition of being. This refers to a basketball player being active, and fluid on the court. The feet are not flat, and the player is on the balls of their feet.

Off-the-Ball Movement: The ability to move without the ball to create open shots, and offensive opportunities.

Open Shot: An uncontested scoring opportunity that a player should hit 90 – 100% of the time.

Outlet Pass: After getting a rebound, the pass made to start movement to towards the opposite end of the floor. The name given to the first pass made on a fast break.

Overhead pass: A pass thrown by an offensive player above the head, usually with both hands.

Palm gap: The space between the basketball and the shooter's hand. About a quarter of an inch of space is appropriate so as, not to allow the ball to come in contact with the shooter's palm.

Pass Ahead: An offensive player who has the ball, passing to a teammate, who is ahead and making a move toward the basket.

Passing Angle: The angle of the pass to another teammate.

Pick: A basketball term to describe an offensive player's move to blocking the movement of a defensive player by standing in a stationary position and letting the defensive player run into them so as to prevent the defensive player from going in their desired direction. of the ball. To avoid being called for a foul, the offensive player setting the pick must remain stationary.

Pick n' Roll: After an offensive player runs his defender through a pick, his/her teammate who set the pick will immediately cut (or roll) to the basket in anticipation of receiving a pass.

Pivot: Rotating the position of oneself by keeping one-foot stationary when in possession of the ball, and rotating left or right.

Pivot foot.

Post-up: When a player positions himself/herself in the key to receive a pass. The player's back is facing the basket and the defensive player is behind or to the side of them.

Practicing Tired: This is making oneself get very tired before working on fundamentals. Learning and practicing under conditions of duress will simulate actual game situation. Real learning takes place when a player is really tired. It is best to put in an intense 1.0 – 1.5 hour practice session before "practicing tired."

Pure Shooter: The term given to a basketball player who has a very high (60% in game situations and 80 – 90% in practice situations) shooting percentage. Some believe this is a natural ability, but in fact it is a learned skill.

Put-Back: Taking grabbing a rebound and shooting the ball immediately back into the basket without bringing the ball below the forehead.

Reach-Around Pass: Passing the basketball using one hand and reaching around the defense to complete the pass.

Rocker Step: A jab or fake step causing that causes the defense to think the offensive player is going to dribble. The offensive player pulls back, and either shoots, drives, or dribbles in the opposite direction.

Roller: *(See "Pick n'Roll)* The offensive player who has set a screen on the defensive player. After successfully "picking," offensive player will open up to the ball and pivoting towards the basket. As the player moves to the basket he will rollout looking for the pass, or alternatively roll towards the basket.

Screen: *(See Pick)* A basketball term to describe an offensive player blocking the movement of a defensive player by standing against the defensive player holding them from going in the direction of the ball. Also called a "pick."

Shooting Through the Ball: This is a concept, which teaches the shooter to understand how the middle and index finger on the shooting hand will follow a direct path to the basket. Imagine the two fingers "going through" the ball and creating backspin.

Shooting Elbow: *(See "Elbow to Elbow")* The practice area located where the free throw line meets the sideline. Shooters use this as a pivot area when practicing shooting drills.

Shooting Window: An imaginary triangle located between the two elbows of the shooter and the bottom of the ball. This allows the player to have a clear, unobstructed view of the court and the basket.

Shot Gap: The most accurate way to measure a players shooting ability.

What is the Shot Gap?: It is the distance between a shooter's wrist bone and the line leading directly to the basket. This is the most accurate way to measure a player's shooting ability. When a player has a wide gap in the shooting hand they usually are not very good shooters.

Spin moves: The ability to make quick and rapid pivots around a the defensive player. This is used used by an offensive player to get open both with and without the basketball.

Skip pass: A bounce pass across the key. Also refers to a long or any pass with one bounce.

Target: The basket, hoop or bucket. In the instance a player is making a pass to a teammate a target can be defined as the object a player shooter is aiming to hit.

Timing-Rhythm-Rotation: *(See page 26)* The part of a basketball shot where the shooter releases the ball at the top of the jump. Having good timing and rotation on the ball allows the shot to be smooth and have great rhythm.

Touch: The part of shooting where the middle, and index finger tips are controlling the shot.

Work Ethic: The ability to work. A player's capacity and desire to work hard to and practice intensely and in order to improve their skills. A player's work ethic is strongly influenced by their attitude. A good work ethic is characterized by one's ability to follow directions and be a self-starter, motivated individual.

Knowing How To Read The Floor

A basketball player should know how to read a basketball court. Understanding the layout of the court and how you can use the lines to gain an advantage over your opponents. If a player does not understand the lines it can be a major disadvantage. There are many traps an unsuspecting player can be lured into by the lines on the basketball court. The various lines drawn on the court are used to control the game. The lines can also be used as a "silent extra player" on the court. Many players do not fully understand the advantages of "reading the court." A solid player will understand how to use the lines to gain an advantage over the opposition.

Suicide Corners. *Never dribble or pick-up your dribble in this area. Always avoid this this part of court.*

Right shooting elbow.

Three Point Line

Base Line

KEY AREA

Half Court Line

Left shooting elbow.

Side Line

These areas are called the **Coffin Corners**. *Never dribble or pick-up your dribble in this area. Always avoid this this part of court. When you have the ball, and you cross the half court line you cannot go back. The side line and the half court line will become two defensive players and you will have placed yourself in a boxed in situation.*

Rules of the Court:
How the lines can be an advantage

- Never dribble the ball along the sidelines
- Never inbound the ball from behind the basket.
- Never step on end line or sideline when in bounding the ball
- Never take one dribble across half court and stop, picking up your dribble.
- Never allow a player to dribble around you by going between you and the sideline or baseline.
  (This is called giving up the baseline or sideline).

Defensive Hint:
By forcing an offensive player to the outside of the court you can create turnovers, which gives your team more offensive opportunities.

Knowing how to use the end lines when passing the ball from out of bounds is one of the most important parts of having great offensive skills.

Offensive team is going this way

Never try to pass an inbounds pass from behind the basket. When the referee hands you the ball be outside the yellow line.

Common lines of a basketball court:

The **Red Zones** are areas an offensive player should avoid at all times. Never stop in these areas with the ball. If you do you give the defense a tremendous advantage. It becomes extremely easy to force a turnover.

The **Green Zones** are areas that are desirable to gaining an advantage over the defense. To be a great offensive player you want to always to be in the **Green Zone**. Always avoiding the **Red Zone**. Avoid picking up your dribble in the **Red Zones** – always stay away form the side-line **Red Zone**.

Knowing How To Read The Half Court

Once the offensive team has crossed the half court line the game takes on a totally separate view. By learning how to read the half court you will be able to identify offensive "lanes of opportunity." The red zones are extremely dangerous places to have the ball. Try to keep the ball in the Green Zones.

Never try to pass an inbounds pass from behind the basket. When the referee hands you the ball be outside the yellow line.

Always pass the ball inbounds from outside the yellow lines.

RIGHT

WRONG

ULTIMATE TARGET ZONE

Common lines of a basketball court:

The **Red Zones** are areas an offensive player should avoid at all times. Never stop in these areas with the ball. If you do you give the defense a tremendous advantage. It becomes extremely easy to force a turnover.

The **Green Zones** are areas that are desirable to gaining an advantage over the defense. To be a great offensive player you want to always to be in the **Green Zone**. Always avoiding the **Red Zone**. Avoid picking up your dribble in the **Red Zones** – always stay away form the side-line **Red Zone**.

Player Self Evaluation

Individual Rating Scale:
CHECK MONTHLY TO SEE IF YOU HAVE IMPROVED

10 – 9 Player has mastered skill and can perform skill at the high school varsity level.

8 – 7 Player needs to work to master this skill, skill has yet to be refined: player could use this skill to a limited degree in a high school varsity game.

6 – 5 This skill is still in the development stage. This skill needs a lot of work before it can be used in competition.

Skill Evaluataion:

Shooting

_____ **Ball position:** Player shoots with ball at least one foot above forehead and in the shooting window, never bringing the ball behind the head.

_____ **Follow-through:** Player allows the middle and index finger to follow a direct path to the basket.

_____ **Rotation:** Player has backspin on the ball and rotation can be detected.

_____ **Feet position on shot:** Players feet are both about shoulder witdth apart and pointing towards the basket.

_____ **Ball speed:** Player has the ability to use ball speed before shot, understands how to set up the defensive player to force them to be off balance.

_____ **Percentage:** Player can shoot: 95% from Zone 1
                                               90% from Zone 2
                                               85% from Zone 3
                                               80% from Zone 4
                                               75% from Zone 5
                                               70% from Zone 6
                                               60% from Zone 7

_____ **Free throws:** Player can make 85% of shots.

_____ **Hand Position:** Help hand is on the side of the ball, not interfering with the shot only use to steady the shot.

_____ **Wrist:** Flexible, and has snap during the follow-through.

Passing

_____ **Ability to see floor and teammates:** Player reads floor, sees open players and completes passes.

_____ **Passes above the shoulders:** Player has ability to use ball speed and can pass with the ball above shoulders and head.

_____ **Can throw left and right handed bounce pass**

_____ **Can throw baseball pass with both left and right hand**

Off Ball Movement

_____ **Ability to set screen:** Ability to make contact and set effective screen.

_____ **Ability to move without ball to get open:** Using spin moves and quick pivots to get open.

Defense

_____ **Man to Man:** Ability to stop player who is dribbling.

_____ **Inside key defense**

_____ **Box out ability**

_____ **Ability to stop baseline drives**

Offense

_____ **Ability to run offense**

_____ **Ability to see open passing lanes**

_____ **Dribbling right**

_____ **Dribbling Left**

_____ **Speed lay-ups**

Work Ethic

_____ **Ability to take instruction**

_____ **Willingness to spend time improving skills**

The Ultimate Off-Season Conditioning Guide

By following this conditioning program, a basketball player can get into peak condition for playing competitive basketball at any level.

A complete physical examine by a medical doctor should be a yearly routine. Always be aware of your medical limitations. **NEVER IGNORE A MEDICAL PROBLEM** – A smart player will not play with injures. Always practice good health.

Quickness and Agility Drills

Simple drills that you can use to increase your speed, balance and explosiveness.

Jump Rope:

This should be part of every basketball players training program. Getting Started requires a good quality jump rope which should be fairly heavy. While jumping rope it is important to not jump more than a few inches off the ground and your arms should remain stationary. Most of the movement should be coming from your toes, wrists and forearms. *(Suggested repetitions: 500 – 1000 a day)*. One-leg *(25 – 50 reps; 3 sets)*; side-to-side with a small hop-step over a line *(100 – 200 reps; 3 sets)*. Incorporate the crossover jump and the double jump (having the rope pass under your feet twice before you land).

Sprints:

Run up and down the court *(baseline to baseline)* Alternate between dribbling the basketball and pure sprints. On the pure sprints, simulate a game situation where you are on defense and pretend that you are running down the court to catch an opponent to prevent them from scoring a lay-up. When dribbling a basketball, sprint *(stay in control)* down the court and make a controlled lay-up.

The Ultimate Individual Full Court Basketball Game

Set a time clock or wrist watch for 8 minutes. This is the first period of a full court game. You are playing this game by yourself. You only get one shot at each end of the court *(no lay-ups)* All shots have to be taken from zone 3 to 7. After a shot you rebound your make or miss and head for the other end of the court. You must dribble with your head up, looking down the court, and never look down at the floor. In between shots you must make at least five spin moves. You also must stop and go using speed dribbles before each shot. Always take the ball to the middle of the court; avoid the sidelines and the baselines. Count each make as 1 point. Your goal is to make 25 shots in the eight minute time period. After 8 minutes take a three-minute break and play the second quarter. Again this is 8 minutes of simulated basketball. After two quarters you get a half time break and return for the final two quarters. The last quarter will be the toughest, but it will simulate a real game in the respect of being fatigued. The ideal goal is to play five of these games a week during the off-season, and two during the season. Work on shots you normally would get in a game. Don't accept a missed shot. You should shoot for perfection.

Uphill Sprints – Find a road nearby with an incline of 10 degrees or more and practice running up it as fast as you can on your toes. Alternate between pure sprints and sprinting while dribbling the ball.

Hop Hurdle *(side-to-side)* – using any object over one foot high and no wider than a foot. Keep your feet together and jump up and over so that when you land you are in position to jump right back over again. You should aim for a total of 25 repetitions. Stay on your toes and keep your feet together. This drill teaches a player how to drive with the knees and toes. Use your arms for momentum as you jump. For added difficulty, keep your hands above your head during the exercise.

Hop Hurdle *(front-to-back)* – repeat the same pattern as in the side to side, but in this exercise you are jumping from front-to-back and then back-to-front over the obstacle. For added difficulty, keep your hands above your head during the exercise.

Strength and Power Drills

A Squats – Using a barbell *(30 – 70 lbs)* or dumbbells *(15 – 35 lbs)* held at shoulder level, lower yourself so that your legs are at a 90 degree angle at the knees and you are keeping your back straight and head up. Do a 2-3 second count on the way down and a 2-3 second count on the way up *(down and up = 1 rep)*. It is more important to do this exercise with lighter weights at higher reps. *(Suggested reps: 25 reps for 3 sets)*

B Lunge scissors – Beginning in a lunge position *(one leg extended out front with the knee at a 90 degree angle and the back leg stretched back so that the knee almost touches the ground)* so the hands are out in front of the chest for balance, "pop" up and shuffle the position of your legs so that when you land, the opposite foot is out front. You do not want to come up too high on the jump. The lower the jump, the faster you have to move the legs and you will build up more strength this way. *(Each jump constitutes a rep and we recommend 3 sets of 25)*

C Dip and Pop – Using a rope or bar *(held in position horizontally at a height of 4 – 5 feet)*, take a 15 - 25 pound dumbbell or medicine ball in your hands and hold it slightly above the shoulders. Squat down so your head is directly underneath the bar or rope and then come up from side to side so that your shoulder touches the bar or rope. *(Suggested reps: 25 reps for 3 sets)*

D Backboard Taps / Slaps - To increase calf strength, jumping capability and explosiveness, practice jumping up and slapping the backboard with both hands in such a motion so that you are not on the ground for more than a split-second between each jump. *(Do sets of 25 repetitions for three sets)*. Once you get comfortable with the motion, practice with a ball in your hands, always keeping the ball above your head and tapping the ball against the backboard each time up. This will teach you to power up to grab rebounds or rise above the defense for a quick two points on the offensive end.

Endurance Drills

A Stair climbing – Run up and down the bleachers in your gymnasium or use a stair-master machine. This will improve your calf strength and increase your stamina. Push yourself until failure.

B Full court game – Simulate a full length game by going as hard as you can up and down the court while practicing spin moves, crossover dribbles, head fakes . . . etc. Incorporate jump shots, runners, lay-ups and any other creative shots you can think of. *(Play 4 eight-minute quarters)*

C Lay-up Marathon – Run up and down the court while dribbling at full speed and practice making ALL your lay-ups and being in position to get the ball when it falls through the hoop. Go as long as you can until you are exhausted.

D Backboard Pinball – Starting on either the right or left block, toss the ball so that it hits the middle part of the top of the square. While the ball is in the air, move over to the opposite block and be in position *(i.e. hands above the head ready to rebound)* to jump up and shoot the ball back to the same spot on the square so that you can run to block you started from and be ready to toss it back again. Make sure your hands are always above the head and ready to catch and toss the ball again.

NOTE: When you do this drill for the first few times, it will be helpful to let the ball bounce once on the other side before you pick it up and put it back. It might take a lot of practice to get the timing down.

Defensive Drills

A **Slide and glide** – Practice staying low and sliding on your feet in the defensive stance. Always keep your palms up and be ready to go for the steal. Be sure to practice the drop-step to simulate instances when the offensive player changes directions.

B **Wall squats** – Position yourself against the wall so that your knees are at a 90 degree angle. You should be on the "balls" of your feet and the heels should not be touching the ground. Hold your hands up in the air or rest them on your head. Do not look down. Hold the position for a minute.
(Repeat for 3 sets)

Food and Diet Considerations

What, when and where you eat and drink has as much of an impact on your overall game as your practice regimen. In order to sustain the energy levels required to perform consistently well at a competitive level, you CANNOT feed your body junk. You need to eat at least 4-5 light meals a day with many snacks in between. Having an energy bar or fruit in between meals is the best way to maintain energy levels and NOT go overboard at any given meal.

DO NOT SKIP BREAKFAST. Breakfast should be your best meal of the day since you will most likely eat it at home and can prepare a good meal. Without going into complicated detail on what your daily food intake should consist of, we will simply provide you with a short list of foods that you should be eating and foods/drinks that you should stay away from.

Recommended foods:

✔ Chicken / steak / fish

✔ Pasta

✔ Potatoes *(not in the form of french fries!)*

✔ Vegetables *(carrots, broccoli, spinach, tomatoes, avocado, string beans, peas, corn . . . etc.)*

✔ Nuts *(i.e. almonds, cashews)*

✔ Fruit

✔ Cottage cheese *(low or non-fat)*

✔ Yogurt *(low or non-fat)*

✔ Oatmeal *(stay away from the ones with brown sugar - - whole oats are the best)*

✔ Wheat bread

✔ Salads

✔ Juices *(i.e. orange, grapefruit, apple . . . etc)*

Things to avoid:

✔ Any fried food *(i.e. french fries, onion rings . . . etc.)*. A good rule of thumb is to stay away from any fast food establishments.

✔ Carbonated beverages *(absolutely no soda)*. The only things you should be drinking are water, fruit juice, milk and sports drinks.

✔ White bread, bagels, donuts, pastries, muffins *(these items are mostly processed carbohydrates and contain little nutritional value)*.

✔ Sweets, candy, chocolate, ice cream . . . etc.

Preparing For College

Getting a scholarship to play basketball in college is very difficult. Usually a college will find players they are interested in way before a player the player becomes interested in their college. Division I coaches begin scouting players in the eight grade. Alumni and boosters often recommend players to various colleges. A high school player's local newspaper usually will get the word out. Word of mouth between coaches and officials usually makes a lot of colleges aware of players who have talent. All division one colleges have assistant coaches that keep notebooks filled with potential recruits. They attend games and keep statistics concerning possible future recruits. These notebooks will have up to 500 potential players and only one or two scholarship will be available. The late bloomer is at a real disadvantage. Many talented players never receive an offer; some players who get scholarships are not the best talent or the most worthy of the scholarship. Writing letters to colleges will get your name on a list of with a thousand other players. Sending a video tape sometimes helps, but most of the tapes are never looked at or if they are it is by some lower level coach who nobody pays any attention to anyway. E-mails, along with letters, will get you on the mailing list, and you will receive the standard form letters. If a college coach wants a player that player will know, the contacts will be frequent, and offers will be made. Contracts or LETTER OF INTENT WILL BE GIVEN.

Division one coaches usually have decided whom they want two to three years prior to a student graduating. They have followed the player's high school career. They all have short list. Most coaches at Division I schools have only a few scholarships to give each year . . . 15 scholarships divided by 4 years= less than four per year. Three to four thousand hopeful high school graduates doesn't offer a big chance for a marginal player.

Every now and then a player who is not recruited by any Division I colleges will make it as a walk on. A walk on pays his way to college and gets a tryout for maybe one spot. The University of Colorado had two spots, and 150 players tried out. MOST WERE VERY GOOD IN HIGH SCHOOL BUT DIDN'T HAVE MUCH OF A CHANCE TO MAKE THE TEAM. The two who did make the team became practice players. They never got into a game. The best way to get noticed is have your high school coach contact the college you are interested in attending. Most college coaches are willing to talk to high school coaches and they will give an indication as to the chances of a potential player getting a look.

Division II colleges are much easier to deal with and players have a much better chance of getting scholarships. The Division II coaches have the same recruiting procedures but the have less talent to choose between and are much more open to players contacting them. The video tape has a better chance of being reviewed, and a Division II coach will usually personally respond to phone calls and letters.

Daily Shooting Drill
Record Form

How to keep track of your shots

Shoot in increments of 25

Place total shots made on top line –

7	12	16	8	total	43	43	Total percent
25	25	25	25		100		

Add across for totals.
Divide shots made by shots taken = Total percent.

Shoot for one minute

Place total shots made on top line –

Shoots made -	68	divide	68	83	Total percent
Shoots taken -	82		82		

Divide shots made by shots taken = Total percent.

Note:
A passing partner is needed for all of these shooting drills.

Elbow to Elbow

___	___	___	___	total ___	___ Total percent
25	25	25	25	100	

___	___	___	___	total ___	___ Total percent
25	25	25	25	100	

Date _____

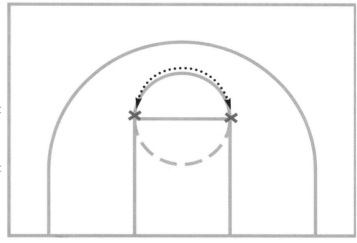

Remember to pivot after each shot.
Before you shoot be square to the basket.

Elbow to Box

___	___	___	___	total ___	___ Total percent
25	25	25	25	100	

___	___	___	___	total ___	___ Total percent
25	25	25	25	100	

Date _____

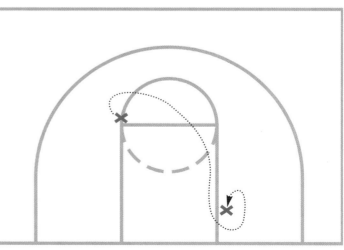

Finesse the short shots and get the head around quickly after
each pivot. Be creative on off-ball movement.

Elbow to Opposite Side of Court

___ ___ ___ ___ total _____ _____ **Total percent**
25 25 25 25   *100*

___ ___ ___ ___ total _____ _____ **Total percent**
25 25 25 25   *100*

Date _____

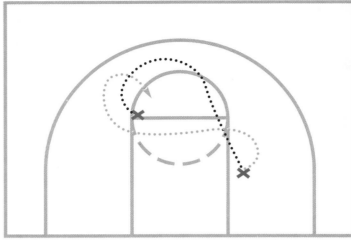

On short shots use backboard. Get a good shooting angle on all shots. Don't accept a missed shot.

Bowtie Drill

___ ___ ___ ___ total _____ _____ **Total percent**
25 25 25 25   *100*

___ ___ ___ ___ total _____ _____ **Total percent**
25 25 25 25   *100*

Date _____

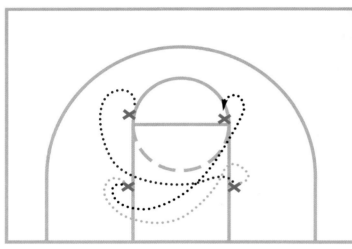

Pivot after each shot, never cross the free throw line only cross at the baseline. Get your head around facing the basket. Keep shoulders square.

Rapid Fire Drill
(Select various location on court)

___ ___ ___ ___ total _____ _____ **Total percent**
25 25 25 25   *100*

___ ___ ___ ___ total _____ _____ **Total percent**
25 25 25 25   *100*

Date _____

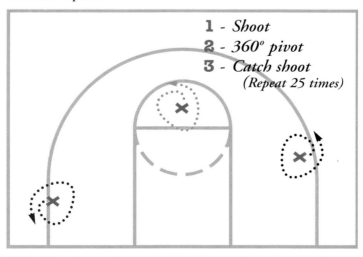

1 - Shoot
2 - 360° pivot
3 - Catch shoot
(Repeat 25 times)

This drill is best with two rebounders, stay in one spot and complete a 360 degree pivot between shot. Ask for each pass and shoot as fast as you can. Make sure each shot is fundamentally sound.

Timed Shooting Drills

One Minute Elbow to Elbow Drill

Shoots made - _____ divide _____ _____ Total percent

Shoots taken -

Shoots made - _____ divide _____ _____ Total percent

Shoots taken -

Date _____

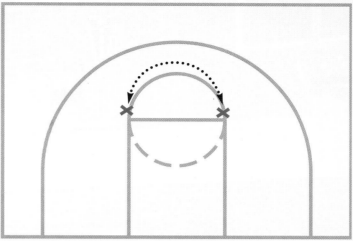

You must keep track of how many shot you take as well as how many you make in one minute. Because these are timed your percentages will drop. Spin after each shot.

One Minute Elbow to Box Drill

Shoots made - _____ divide _____ _____ Total percent

Shoots taken -

Shoots made - _____ divide _____ _____ Total percent

Shoots taken -

Date _____

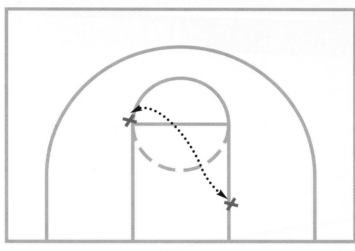

Make sure you go at game speed, pivot after each shot. This drill will teach you how to shoot a long shot and then a short shot.

One Minute Rapid Fire Spin Drill *(Change location after each minute)*

Shoots made - _____ divide _____ _____ Total percent

Shoots taken -

Shoots made - _____ divide _____ _____ Total percent

Shoots taken -

Date _____

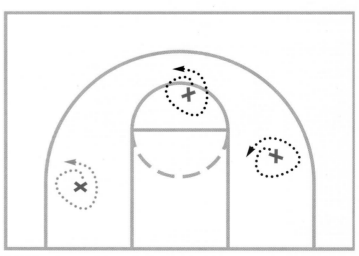

Work to increase the number you can make in one minute. Alternate spots on the floor always stay within your shooting range.

Big Time Shooting drills

Super Fifty

_____ total _____ _____ Total percent
    50   50

_____ total _____ _____ Total percent
    50   50

Date _____

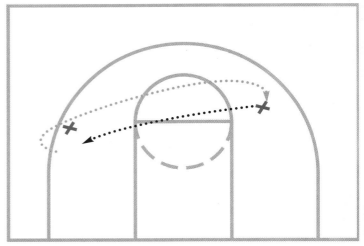

Select two spots in zone 4 or 5. Pivot after each shot. At full speed shoot 50 shots in a row without stopping.

Super One Hundred

_____ total _____ _____ Total percent
   100   100

_____ total _____ _____ Total percent
   100   100

Date _____

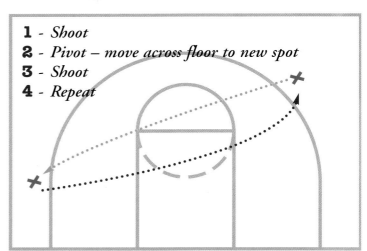

1 - *Shoot*
2 - *Pivot – move across floor to new spot*
3 - *Shoot*
4 - *Repeat*

Select two spots on the floor and alternate between these spot using pivots. It is best to use areas where you have a difficult time making shots. By shooting one hundred shots in a row you will become fatigued and you will simulate game conditions. The last 25 shots will be the toughest. These will teach you the most.

Note:
Having a good passing partner to throw crisp passes is a must.

Dealing With The Team Concept

Maintaining a positive relationship with your teammates and coach is very important. By demonstrating maturity and leadership, your teammates will respect you and you will build trust with your coach.

To build this trust and respect, try doing the following:

- Always arrive at practice on time and try to get there early to work on the skills you need to perfect. This shows you are a dedicated team player who takes the game and your team seriously.

- Try to stay after practice, when you are tired, as this is the best time to work on skills that are most similar to game situations *(free throws, jump shots)*.

- Never show emotion. This can be difficult, especially when you are fatigued. The second you begin to show emotion or get frustrated, you will chip away at the confidence and trust you had built up with your teammates and coach.

Getting along with your coach:

Your coach dictates your playing time. You should always try your best to maintain a positive relationship with him/her, so your playing time will not be affected by anything besides your skills. Maintaining a positive relationship may be difficult, but you must try extremely hard to keep things on a positive note.

If you have a difficult time getting along with your coach, your playing time may be reduced. There are many different types of coaches in the game of basketball and each has their own method of preparing a team for competition. Do your best to understand what your coach is trying to accomplish and work to fit into his/her system.

Getting along with your teammates:

- Understand strengths and weaknesses of your teammates.

- Don't criticize your teammates for any weaknesses they may have.

- Always be supportive and never resort to personal insults at any time.

- Work to correct the mistakes you make in practice and make sure you learn your team's offense and defense. Study each and every aspect of your offense(s) and know your role and the roles of every other player.

How to select the best Summer Basketball Camp

How you spend your summer months will likely dictate how you perform during the season. One of the key elements of your summer itinerary may include a trip to a weeklong summer basketball camp or two. Make sure you have thoroughly researched your camp to ensure you get the most for your money.

Here is what to keep in mind when selecting a camp:

- Level of individual instruction by an experienced coach *(coach to player ratio no greater than 10 to 1)*.

- Amount of time spent on instruction and clinics vs. playing games and scrimmages. Some camps consist of an hour or two of instruction in the morning followed by afternoon and evening games. At camps like these you will not get the learning experience nor the level of practice you are looking for since most of your time will be spent playing or waiting to play games

- Big name basketball star camps. Any professional player who puts on a camp will charge a lot of money and deliver a poor camp from an instructional standpoint. The star will usually show up for an hour or two in the morning and then turn the camp over to other coaches who will just supervise games. *(Don't be star struck - find a camp that teaches)*.

- Big name college camps: Any college program that puts on a camp will be better than a professional superstar camp. However, it is still a camp that fills most of the time with scrimmages. If the camp is big, youíre wasting your time. Summers are for working on skills. You will not get the gym time at a big camp. You would be better off to join a private gym and work on individual skills.

- Avoid outside basketball camps. If you have to be outside for instruction, or play games on asphalt courts you could experience more harm than good.

To get the most out of your summer basketball camp, choose a camp that focuses on instruction and clinics as opposed to a camp that draws 300 – 500 players and is nothing more than a summer income for a basketball coach. Be selective, choose a camp that will help you develop your basketball skills.

How To Be A Great Competitor

- *Never complain about another teammate.*

- *Never show emotion.*

- *Never display anger.*

- *Never talk to a player on the other team.*

- *Never complain about an official's call; they never change the call and you are only wasting your breath.*

- *Always pay attention to the time and score.*

- *Always know how many fouls you have and time outs are left.*

- *Never under estimate your competition; someone will always surprise you.*

- *If you are a winner on the court you will be a winner off the court.*

- *Your education is first and foremost; if you don't take care of your grades, basketball will be meaningless.*

ALPINE
BASKETBALL

SHOOTERS ACADEMY

AT LAKE TAHOE
INCLINE VILLAGE NEVADA

The Alpine Sports Basketball Shooters Academy is exclusively for junior high, high school and college players. This shooting Academy is designed as a high intensity, high discipline learning experience. This camp will cover all the drills and skills illustrated in this book. Each athlete will receive intense personalized instruction. A one-week session will drastically improve the athlete's ability to score. All players are screened prior to acceptance. Once accepted into this program, players will learn how to develop precision shooting and explosive accuracy. A strong and positive work ethic is required from all attending athletes. Each session has a limited enrollment which guarantees a high level of individualized instruction. Athletes can expect to spend eight to ten hours per day working on their shooting skills, as well as all aspects of offensive basketball.

If you are interested in attending one of the shooting camps, write to us for more information. You will be sent an application form and a schedule of summer camps.

For more information write to:

Alpine Sports
P.O. Box 186 • Crystal Bay, Nevada 89402

alpinesports@earthlink.net

Dedicated to my loving family, for their support in making this book a reality.

About The Author

Frank Wright has coached at the high school and college level for the past 30 years. Frank travels across the United States and Canada teaching the art of shooting and offensive skills. Since founding the Alpine Basketball Camps in Lake Tahoe, Nevada, 15 years ago, over 15,000 players have attended his camps. Frank has a keen passion for the sport of basketball and a unique understanding of fundamentals needed to be a great shooter. His teaching has helped thousands of players correct their shots. Through his instruction, many players have taken their skills to the next level. Frank is a widely regarded authority on basketball fundamentals, especially shooting. Through the years he has assisted coaches at all levels in developing shooting programs for their teams. By writing this book, Frank hopes to make it possible for any basketball player to develop shooting skills that are fundamentally correct.

Acknowledgements

Art Director
> Andrew Garcia

Editing
> Kathlee Coleman
> David Wright
> Lou Poggi

Printing
> Asia Pacific Offset Ltd.

Athletic Demonstrations:
> David Wright
> Zack Koebel
> Cody Johnson
> Cory Johnson

Special Thanks to:
> Art and Mel Johnson
> Pacific Printing
> Mike Posey
> Tionna Cunningham
> Alona Fuchs